An Invisible Minority

REVISED AND EXPANDED EDITION

UNIVERSITY PRESS OF FLORIDA

Florida A&M University, Tallahassee
Florida Atlantic University, Boca Raton
Florida Gulf Coast University, Ft. Myers
Florida International University, Miami
Florida State University, Tallahassee
New College of Florida, Sarasota
University of Central Florida, Orlando
University of Florida, Gainesville
University of North Florida, Jacksonville
University of South Florida, Tampa
University of West Florida, Pensacola

An Invisible Minority

Brazilians in New York City

REVISED AND EXPANDED EDITION

Maxine L. Margolis

University Press of Florida
Gainesville/Tallahassee/Tampa/Boca Raton
Pensacola/Orlando/Miami/Jacksonville/Ft. Myers/Sarasota

14 13 12 11 10 09   6 5 4 3 2 1

Library of Congress Cataloging-in-Publication Data
Margolis, Maxine L., 1942–
An invisible minority: Brazilians in New York City/Maxine L.
Margolis.—Rev. and expanded ed.
p. cm.
Includes bibliographical references and index.
ISBN 978-0-8130-3323-5 (alk. paper)
1. Brazilian Americans—New York (State)—New York—Social
conditions. 2. Brazilians—New York (State)—New York—Social
conditions. 3. Immigrants—New York (State)—New York—Social
conditions. 4. Brazil—Emigration and immigration. 5. New York
(N.Y.)—Emigration and immigration. 6. New York (N.Y.)—Ethnic
relations. I. Title.
F128.9.B68M35 2009
304.8'74710819–dc22 2008035072

The University Press of Florida is the scholarly publishing agency for the
State University System of Florida, comprising Florida A&M University,
Florida Atlantic University, Florida Gulf Coast University, Florida
International University, Florida State University, New College of Florida,
University of Central Florida, University of Florida, University of North
Florida, University of South Florida, and University of West Florida.

University Press of Florida
15 Northwest 15th Street
Gainesville, FL 32611–2079
http://www.upf.com

For Jerry
With much love and gratitude

Contents

Preface   ix

1. A New Ingredient in the Melting Pot   1

2. Brazilian Immigrants: A Portrait   23

3. Working New York   38

4. Immigrant Life in Gotham City   69

5. Ethnicity, Race, and Gender   92

6. From Sojourner to Settler   106

Postscript: Brazilian Immigrants and September 11, 2001   121

Notes   131

References   135

Index   147

Preface

Brazilian immigrants in New York City are the focus of this book. But it is about more than one particular immigrant group, because the story of Brazilians illustrates many of the debates that surround immigration to the United States today:

- Who are the new immigrants and what attracts them to this country?
- What kind of jobs do they hold and what niche do immigrants fill in the American economy?
- Are immigrants taking jobs away from native-born workers?
- Why the outcry against immigration to the United States?
- What about the hot button issue of illegal immigration?
- Do all undocumented immigrants fit the standard stereotype of rural, uneducated people fleeing poverty and lives of desperation?

While this book is about Brazilian immigrants, it is also an account of undocumented immigration. About 50 percent of the Brazilians I met in New York during my original study in the early 1990s were undocumented; by 2000 up to 70 percent of Brazilians in the greater New York metropolitan area lacked work papers. And so, questions related to this controversial issue became one of my research interests. I wanted to know how Brazilians became undocumented, how they secured visas to come to the United States, how they entered the country, and what it was like to live "out of status," that is, as an immigrant who is working in the United States illegally. But it is important to emphasize that nothing I relate in the pages to follow is unique to Brazilians in terms of their undocumented standing. Brazilians represent undocumented immigrants of diverse national origins. As such, they serve as surrogates for many other "out of status" immigrant groups with powerful economic motives for living in this country.

We will also see that this is a tale that contradicts the prevailing American stereotype of the "illegal alien"[1] as a young, unschooled male who comes from an impoverished village in Mexico. From the earliest days of my research in New York City, I realized that the Brazilian immigrants I was interviewing had little in common with the exemplary "illegal" of contemporary American discourse. Most of the Brazilians seeking their fortune in this country during the 1990s were middle and lower middle class and many had university educations. And so this also became a narrative about a new kind of immigrant, an immigrant who was not fleeing from dire poverty or political repression. Rather, Brazilians, like many immigrants now arriving in this country, are economic refugees escaping their nation's chaotic economy. Moreover, many claim to be sojourners, not settlers—immigrants who are in this country temporarily, visitors who will only stay long enough to save money to be used after the return home.

The Brazilian immigrant experience bears many parallels to that of other immigrant groups, but it is also uniquely their own. Throughout this book I will describe features of Brazilian society that help decipher the culture clashes and stresses and strains that particularly mark the Brazilian encounter with immigrant status. Here I have drawn on my own familiarity with Brazilian culture and my extensive experience doing field work in Brazil and among Brazilian immigrants in Paraguay.

The research for this book was done in several phases. During the first phase, which lasted several weeks, I did an informal survey and open-ended interviews with about fifty Brazilians, including both recent immigrants and long-term residents of New York City. Through these interviews I became familiar with the general contours of Brazilian immigration to the city, its history, the neighborhoods in which Brazilians live, and the kind of jobs they hold. I then drew up a series of questions that I wanted to answer in my research.

I gathered much of my data during the next phase, a twelve-month period in the early 1990s when I lived in New York City while on sabbatical from the University of Florida. I selected informants and filled out one hundred questionnaires on a sample of them. The questionnaires covered most aspects of Brazilian immigrant life, from the decision to migrate to New York to Brazilians' subsequent experiences working and living in the city. A series of questions were meant to profile the immigrants—their vital statistics, hometowns, social and educational backgrounds, and prior work histories.

Choosing the subjects for the questionnaires became a major dilemma because, for obvious reasons, it is extremely difficult to estimate the size of populations that are partly composed of undocumented immigrants (Cornelius 1982). This was certainly true of Brazilians in New York City. The majority of Brazilians did not participate in the U.S. censuses of 1990 and 2000, and no other reliable quantitative data is available on them. As a result, the number of Brazilians residing in New York City was and still is unknown, as was their residential distribution in the metropolitan area. Thus, there is no sampling frame for selecting individuals from this population, making it impossible to come up with a random sample of Brazilian immigrants in the city.

Snowball sampling, a non-random sampling technique, was used instead because it has proved to be useful in contacting "hidden" populations, such as undocumented immigrants (Cornelius 1982; Bernard 2005). Snowball sampling uses informants' own networks of friends and relatives to create a sample. I used it in the following way: after making initial contacts with a few Brazilian immigrants, I asked each one for the names of one or two other Brazilians who might agree to be interviewed. These, in turn, were asked for additional names; the process continued, and a network of informants was created.

The drawback of snowball sampling is that the data gathered cannot be generalized beyond the sample at hand. In other words, the statistical portrait of Brazilians presented in this book should be seen only as a useful guide because the sample on which it is based was not drawn randomly. However, keeping these limitations in mind, snowball sampling can still be a very credible research tool when combined with qualitative ethnographic techniques.

Aside from the subjects of the questionnaires, I had informal conversations with dozens and dozens of other Brazilians—more than 250 in all—while doing what anthropologists call "participant observation." During all phases of the research, I visited peoples' homes and attended concerts and sporting events. I went to church services and street fairs and spent time at stores, restaurants, and nightclubs frequented by Brazilians. I also visited some Brazilians at work. In short, I tried to immerse myself in the daily life of New York's Brazilian immigrant community.

During this initial phase of research, I also spent three weeks in Brazil, where I interviewed officials of the American consulate in Rio de Janeiro and some returned migrants. I traveled to the city of Governador Valadares in the state of Minas Gerais, a major exporter of *brazucas*, as Brazilians living in the United States are called. I talked to a few dozen people there—local officials, travel agents, families with relatives in the United States—and collected data on the history and impact of the emigrant flow. Insights and data from this and subsequent stays in Brazil appear throughout the book.

In the most recent phase of research I have tried to generalize about the Brazilian immigrant experience in the United States by visiting Brazilian communities in Boston and Framingham, Massachusetts, Danbury, Connecticut, and Newark, New Jersey, and by talking with immigrants and community leaders there. And in 2007, accompanied by Ambassador José Alfredo Graça Lima, the Brazilian consul general in New York, I was able to visit a functioning "itinerant consulate" serving the Brazilian immigrant community in Danbury.[2]

I have also included the findings of researchers in these and other U.S. communities with significant Brazilian populations and have read the vast and growing scholarly literature on Brazilian immigration to the United States. Book-length studies have now been done on Brazilian immigrants in Massachusetts and California, and edited volumes report on Brazilian communities elsewhere in the United States. Relevant news reports in both the U.S. and Brazilian media are also cited.

Finally, I have updated demographic and other data and have drawn on recent research to chart the ongoing flow of Brazilians into the United States, including new routes of entry. I have also included new information on Brazilian immigration to the United States found in American and Brazilian newspaper articles and at internet sites.

All of this information is incorporated in the present book, which is a revised, updated, and expanded version of earlier studies (Margolis 1994, 1998a). In a postscript for this edition, I have analyzed the impact on Brazilian immigrants of the attacks on New York City and Washington, D.C., on September 11, 2001.

Several people contributed to this book. The research and insights of Ana Cristina Braga Martes on Brazilians in Boston gave me an invaluable comparative perspective on Brazilian immigration to the United States. Martes was also a lively and instructive guide to the Brazilian community in the Boston area, as were Heloisa Galvão, Antonio Souza, and Luciano Tosta. I learned a great deal as well in informal conversations with Roberto Lima and Bispo Filho, editors of the *Brazilian Voice*, published in Newark, N.J.; with Fausto Mendes da Rocha, the executive director of the Brazilian Immigrant Center in Allston, Massachusetts; and with Ambassador José Alfredo Graça Lima, the Brazilian consul general in New York, to whom I am particularly grateful. Many dozens of Brazilians in New York helped me with both my initial and subsequent research and generously shared their experiences as immigrants with me. Most recently, these have included Eloah Teixeira and Marcia Martins. I want to single out Tereza Costa, a former social services representative at the Brazilian consulate in New York

City, for her research insights. I also thank my economists-in-residence, Nicola Cetorelli and Michele Gambera, for their internet-mediated assistance finding data on the Brazilian economy, and Charles Wood of the University of Florida for locating updated data on race. And finally, as always, I am genuinely grateful to JTM, to whom this work is dedicated, not only for his general research and editorial and photographic assistance, but also for his TLC while I was writing and revising this book.

A New Ingredient in the Melting Pot

In March 2005 television sets all over Brazil were tuned to the new eve-
ning soap opera *América*, the saga of a woman's journey from Brazil to the
United States via Mexico. After having been denied a U.S. tourist visa and
making two unsuccessful attempts at entering the country, the soap opera's
Brazilian heroine finally makes her way across the Mexican border into the
United States by hiding in the back of a truck. Spurred on by the dream of
helping to give her poor family a better life back in Brazil, she travels to
Miami where she works as a housecleaner, a baby sitter, and eventually, a
go-go dancer.

At about the same time that *América* went on the air, Brazil's Ministry
of Foreign Affairs estimated that nearly 2 million Brazilians were living
abroad, with the largest number—somewhere between 800,000 and 1.1
million—living in the United States. Over the last decade or so, the theme
of Brazilians abroad was also widely echoed in stories in the nation's news-
magazines, which proclaimed that there was a "Brazilian Exodus" and gave
details of the "Brazilian Diaspora" (Salgado 2001; Lucena 1996).

This is certainly a surprise. After all, when Americans think of immigrants in New York City or other parts of the United States, Mexicans, Hai-
tians, Cubans, and Central Americans or even Koreans or Indians are likely
to come to mind. But Brazilians? Most Americans associate Brazil with
tropical forests, World Cup soccer, *bossa nova* music, and sunny beaches
awash with bronzed, scantily clad bathers, but certainly not with immigrants to this country. But the fact is that beginning in the mid-1980s as
the Brazilian economy went into a tailspin, untold numbers of Brazilians
migrated to the United States, Canada, Japan, Australia, and various countries in Europe (Margolis 2004). Yet it is also true that until quite recently
Brazilians did not think of themselves as immigrants because they had had
no experience with immigration. As one Brazilian put it: "We have not been
immigrants since the Portuguese discovered Brazil in 1500. They discovered it and then they just sat there."

Governador Valadares: A Sending Community

Scattered enclaves of Brazilians have long existed in the United States. Where Brazil's pioneer immigrants to the United States first settled is unknown, but as early as the mid- and late 1960s, there were small Brazilian communities in New York City, the Catskill Mountain region of New York State, Newark, New Jersey, Boston, and California. Some of the first Brazilian immigrants to arrive in the United States came from Governador Valadares, a city of some 270,000 in the state of Minas Gerais in south central Brazil. Valadarenses—as natives of the city are called—still make up a major segment of the Brazilian population in the Boston area, Newark, and in some towns in Connecticut and south Florida. In fact, emigrants from various parts of Minas Gerais are well represented in Brazilian communities throughout the United States.

An intriguing question is why such a disproportionate share of Brazil's pioneer emigrants come from a single city and its surrounding towns in the interior of Brazil. Why has Governador Valadares become an emigrant-sending community with perhaps forty thousand of its citizens living in the United States and assorted European countries at any given time? This is a place where over half of the population has a relative in the United States or Europe, a community whose sons and daughters send an estimated $72 million back home annually (Beraba 2007; Rohter 2005; Mineo 2006a).

While large-scale emigration from Governador Valadares only began in the 1980s, it has deeper roots that can be traced back to World War II. It was then that the long period of contact between the city and the United States began. During the war Brazil became the world's leading producer of mica, at that time a critical material for insulation. Mica was mined in the state of Minas Gerais and the major mining and processing centers were located in and around Governador Valadares. After the war the industry waned, but the stage had been set for future emigration from the city because mica was responsible for the American presence there. Some Americans were associated with various aspects of the industry, while others came to the city to work with Brazil's national public health service. Because of the community's role as a mining center for materials needed in the war effort, a public health office was set up to combat malaria. Both public health concerns and the mica industry brought American medical personnel and engineers to town, and some hired Valadarenses as household servants.

Local tradition has it that when these Americans were living in Governador Valadares they often paid with dollar bills—for shoeshines, taxi rides, sandwiches—and rarely asked for change. Since in those days the equivalent of a dollar bill in Brazilian currency was quite a lot of money, townspeople became convinced that, as the saying goes, money must grow on trees in the United States. This is why when the Americans returned home after the war and invited some of their local employees to go with them, the invitations were readily accepted. Such is the tale of how emigrants from Governador Valadares first came to the United States (Margolis 1990).

Today a culture of out-migration exists in Governador Valadares and the surrounding towns, a culture found in communities that have extensive, long established patterns of international migration; children in them grow up expecting to migrate as part of their life experience. As such, many young Valadarenses plan to migrate to the United States instead of working on the family farm or going on to college. In fact, educators in town are concerned about the lack of ambition among the children of immigrants to the United States who see no reason to pursue a career when they expect to migrate as well. And so the continued draw of dollars and the long tradition of emigration have made Governador Valadares the "emigrant capital of Brazil." So many townspeople now live in the United States, according to a local joke, that only the mayor has stayed behind to turn out the lights when he leaves (Margolis 1990; Mineo 2006b).

The small pioneer enclaves of Valadarenses and other Brazilians in the United States remained relatively unknown in Brazil and received virtually no news coverage there. During the 1970s and early 1980s the rate of emigration from Brazil began a slow but steady increase; then from the mid-1980s on it soared. Tens of thousands of Brazilians headed for New York, New Jersey, Connecticut, Massachusetts, Florida, and California, and these same states remain the primary areas of Brazilian residence in the United States today. They are home to some three-quarters of the Brazilians currently living in this country. Smaller Brazilian enclaves are found in Chicago, Philadelphia, Washington, D.C., Atlanta, Houston and, most recently, New Orleans.

The greater New York metropolitan area is home to one of the largest Brazilian populations in the United States. Aside from New York City itself, a number of Brazilian nuclei dot the region. Brazilians live in Westchester, a suburban county just north of the city, and in the town of Mineola on Long Island. Newark and several smaller cities in New Jersey are also now home to sizeable Brazilian communities, as are the Connecticut towns of Danbury, Waterbury, and Bridgeport.

Boston, including its suburbs and the towns south and west of the city, is also a major destination for Brazilian immigrants, as is Cape Cod. In fact, in recent years Brazilians have become the fastest growing immigrant population in Massachusetts, accounting for 20 percent of new arrivals. In some communities in the region the Brazilian presence cannot be overlooked. To cite just one example, in the town of Framingham just west of Boston, the estimated fifteen thousand Brazilians living there account for over 20 percent of the local population (Abraham 2005b; Gedan 2002).

Moving away from the Northeast, central and southern Florida are also sites of Brazilian settlement, and some call the small community of Pompano Beach the "Brazilian immigrant capital of south Florida" (Resende 2002). Then, too, in recent years Brazilians have been moving to Atlanta and its suburbs, places not usually associated with immigrant settlement (Pickel 2000; Marcus 2008). And since 2005, untold numbers of Brazilians have gone to New Orleans to work in post-Katrina reconstruction (Kaste 2006; Gibson 2008; Nolan 2008). Finally, on the West Coast, Los Angeles, San Diego, and especially San Francisco have burgeoning Brazilian enclaves (Beserra 2003; Ribeiro 1999).

Brazilians in Gotham

If you were to visit New York City and ask any native New Yorker how to get to Little Italy or Chinatown, you would be quickly directed to take the subway or a taxi downtown to either of these well-known tourist sites. But if you were to inquire how to get to Little Brazil, you would be met with a puzzled look. "Little Brazil? What's that?" would be the likely response. The reason for the puzzled look is that New York has no distinct Brazilian residential neighborhood, no area that is comparable to Chinatown or Little Italy. Moreover, the single commercial street in Manhattan—East 46th Street—that caters to Brazilian tourists and immigrants and which they call "Little Brazil" is virtually unknown to other residents of the city, despite the fact that since 1996 official signs at either end of the street have proclaimed it "Little Brazil."

Much of the city's sizeable Brazilian population actually lives in Queens, more specifically in Astoria and neighboring Long Island City, traditional working-class neighborhoods with large Greek, Italian, South Asian, and Hispanic populations. In fact, 60 percent of the Brazilian immigrants I studied lived in Queens, with the majority in Astoria.[1] Aside from Brazilians, Astoria is also home to other recent arrivals: Filipinos, Bangladeshis,

Indians, Chinese, and Irish. It is an attractive locale to Brazilians and other immigrants new to the city because of its proximity to Manhattan, where most have jobs, and its relatively inexpensive rents.

Astoria is a neighborhood of low-rise apartment buildings, modest attached two-family houses, and the dominating presence of an elevated subway line that shrouds its main commercial thoroughfare in constant gloom. But despite its ethnic diversity, there are occasional clues to the Brazilian presence there—the odd Brazilian flag poking out of an apartment window, the cramped shops stocked with Brazilian food products, newspapers, magazines, and videos, and the travel agencies featuring inexpensive flights to Rio de Janeiro and São Paulo. Aside from Manhattan's Little Brazil, Astoria is the only place in New York City that has a cluster of Brazilian-owned businesses—grocery stores, remittance and travel agencies, call car companies, a unisex beauty salon, and several bars and eating places—catering to the needs of the immigrant community.

Numbers, Numbers, Numbers

The most questionable feature of Brazilian immigration to the United States is its size. It is impossible to gauge with any degree of certainty how many Brazilians live in New York City or other cities in the United States or in the country as a whole. The problem can be illustrated with just a few figures. The 2000 U.S. census recorded only 14,240 Brazilians in New York City, with 51,500 in the New York metropolitan region. That same year the local Brazilian consulate estimated that 350,000 Brazilians were living in the greater New York metropolitan area! Or take the widely differing estimates for Massachusetts. According to the 2000 U.S. census, Massachusetts was home to 36,669 Brazilians, but the Brazilian government estimated that there were 225,000 Brazilians in the Boston consular district at the start of the millennium (Lobo and Salvo 2004).

And the situation is no clearer at the national level. By 2005 the Brazilian government was estimating that about 1.1 million Brazilians were living in the United States. But one would never know the size of the Brazilian population by looking at the figures from the 2000 U.S. census, which managed to count a mere 212,000 Brazilians in the entire country, or from the more recent 2007 American Community Survey, which only located some 339,000 Brazilians living in the United States. These contradictions are summarized by comparing the figures in tables 1.1 and 1.2.

Aside from numbers, another noteworthy demographic phenomenon is

Table 1.1. Foreign-Born Brazilians in the United States, 2000

Florida	44,536
Massachusetts	36,669
California	22,931
New York	22,265
New Jersey	22,097
Connecticut	10,379
Texas	6,915
Georgia	5,144
Maryland	4,697
Illinois	3,488
Pennsylvania	3,264
Virginia	2,803
All Other States	27,240
Total	212,428

Source: 2000 U.S. Census, Summary File 3, PCT 19

Table 1.2. Brazilians in Brazilian Consular Districts in the United States, 2005

New York	350,000
Houston	300,000
Boston	225,000
Miami	150,000
Los Angeles	40,000
San Francisco	30,000
Chicago	12,000
Total	1,107,000

Source: Itamaraty, Divisão de Assistência Consular, 2005

the expansion of the Brazilian population in the United States from metropolitan areas in the Northeast, Florida, and the West Coast to smaller communities, including ones that are not usually associated with immigrant settlement. For example, there is a burgeoning Brazilian population in Atlanta and its suburbs—perhaps numbering as many as thirty thousand—as well as Brazilian communities in such unlikely places as Goose Creek and Mount Pleasant, South Carolina (Marcus 2008; Goyette 2008; White 2008).

Not only are Brazilians settling in a greater variety of locales in the United States, but in recent years many have become involved in secondary migrations both within and across state lines. The moves are made because of job availability, the cost of rent, or considerations of climate. Some Brazilians have moved from New York City to New Jersey, Connecticut, and Pennsylvania, while in New Jersey others have left Newark to take jobs in smaller communities in the state. In Massachusetts Brazilians now live throughout the commonwealth, not just in the Boston metropolitan area. Then, too, many Brazilians in southern Florida are secondary migrants who lived in the Northeast before moving to the Sunshine State, which many say they prefer because of the weather (Jansen and Siqueira 2005; Suarez 2003; Siqueira and Lourenço 2004).

Why Are They Invisible?

Why are the figures for Brazilians living in the United States so divergent? Why are estimates of the number of Brazilians in this country five or six times greater than the number recorded in official census statistics? The major reason for these contradictory figures is that a significant but unknown percentage of Brazilians living in the United States are undocumented immigrants. In New York City, for example, just over half of the Brazilians I studied in the early 1990s were undocumented, and more recent estimates suggest that up to 70 percent of Brazilian immigrants in this country may lack papers. Finally, according to the Department of Homeland Security, the number of undocumented Brazilians in the United States grew by 70 percent between 2000 and 2005. Most arrive in the United States on tourist visas, take jobs, overstay their visas, and thereby become undocumented. Immigrants who are in the United States illegally—no matter what their nationality—try to maintain a low profile and, in doing so, are very difficult to count.

Aside from the issue of legal status, I also found that many Brazilians simply were not interested in participating in the U.S. census. As we will see in the pages to follow, most Brazilians—at least initially—view their stay in the United States as temporary. They think of themselves as sojourners in this country rather than as true immigrants. Given the transitory nature of their residence, they see nothing to gain and possibly something to lose by making their presence known by filling out official census forms (Margolis 1995a).

Yet another reason why Brazilians have been consistently undercounted in the U.S. census and other studies that classify and tally immigrants is their vague race or ethnicity. The classification of Brazilians is problematic because they do not fit easily into any standard American ethnic or racial category. They cannot be classified as "Hispanic"—a category used in the census and in other statistical surveys—because they speak Portuguese, not Spanish.

But aren't Brazilians Latinos? Not according to the U.S. census. For the first time in the 2000 census the Latino category specifically *excluded* Brazilians, and Brazilians who checked Hispanic/Latino and wrote in "Brazilian" were marked "not Hispanic/Latino" and their nationality went unnoted. And while Brazilians are "Latin Americans" this is a geographical designation, not an ethnic one. Then, too, using racial instead of ethnic terms also leaves the issue unresolved because the Brazilian population is neither black nor white; Brazilians may be either "race" or any shade in between (Marrow 2002).

Here is an example of how some of these issues come into play in assigning ethnic identity: A professor of Portuguese at Brown University was asked to give a talk to Portuguese-speaking children at several public schools in the Boston area. He assumed that they were the children of emigrants from Portugal since there has long been a Portuguese community in the region. But as soon as he arrived at the first school and heard the children's accents, he immediately realized that 90 to 95 percent of the children were Brazilian, *not* Portuguese. The same ratio held for the other classrooms he visited at different grade levels. The bilingual education teachers were aware that the children in their classes were from Brazil not Portugal, but the schools never informed state authorities who fund the classes because most of the Brazilians are children of undocumented immigrants; by simply referring to them as "Portuguese speakers" their legal status did not become an issue.

As a result of these factors, Brazilians are invisible even when compared to other undocumented immigrant groups in the United States. For example, despite the high percentage of undocumented individuals in the Brazilian community, the Department of Homeland Security's estimates of the resident unauthorized alien population in the United States do not place Brazil in the top twenty countries of origin, thus implying a resident population of fewer than thirty thousand undocumented Brazilians in the entire country, a ridiculously low figure that bears no relation to reality. Perhaps, however, within this context, there is an advantage to being "invisible."

Why Do They Come?

While there are doubts as to the actual number of Brazilian immigrants living in the United States, there is little question about what motivates them to leave Brazil and seek their fortune abroad. Brazilians in the United States often describe themselves as "economic refugees" or "economic prospectors" and these images are born out in my own study. Nearly two-thirds of the immigrants I interviewed in New York City cited economic or professional reasons for coming to this country. There are two sides to the equation that explain the economic motivations of Brazilian immigrants: on the one side are the factors that prodded them to leave Brazil in the first place, and on the other are the conditions that led them to immigrate to the United States.

Brazil has long been beset by endemic economic problems—low wages, underemployment, a high cost of living, economic insecurity, and until 1994, hyperinflation. The chaotic economic situation in Brazil is evident from a few statistics: since 1980 Brazil has had four currencies, five wage and price freezes, nine economic stabilization programs, and an inflation index of 146 *million percent* (Brooke 1993)! But it is not these lifeless statistics that cause Brazilians to leave their homeland, but the real-life conditions that arise from them.

During the first decade of significant emigration from Brazil—roughly 1984 to 1994—a major culprit in the exodus was the nation's out of control inflation. Always high, inflation soared during the late 1980s and early 1990s, reaching over 2,500 percent annually by 1994, a rate of 40 percent a month. To make some sense of these figures, consider the following: if the Brazilian currency had not been adjusted to keep up with inflation, a *cafezinho* (a Brazilian-style espresso) that cost 15 *cruzeiros* in 1980 would have sold for 22 billion *cruzeiros* by mid-1993 (Brooke 1993, 1994a, 1994b).[2]

In 1994 the Brazilian government instituted an economic plan that brought down the rate of inflation. But then prices for goods and services skyrocketed and within a year the Brazilian media was awash with stories about how middle-class Brazilians were suffering under the new economic program; one headline read "The Middle Class Passes from Euphoria to Bankruptcy" (Peluso and Goldberg 1995). While general inflation was up 35 percent annually—low by Brazilian standards—for the Brazilian middle class it had actually risen by 56 percent. Higher prices for services used primarily by the middle class were to blame. Rent was up over 200 percent; domestic service, 150 percent; restaurant meals, 66 percent; medical care, 60 percent; and school fees, nearly 50 percent. Then, too, goods bought by average middle-class Brazilians also rose and became far more expensive than they were in the United States: a can of Coke cost about 50 percent more in Rio de Janeiro than in Washington D.C.; a Sony CD player, 350 percent more; and Reebok sneakers almost 400 percent more (*Veja* 1995b; Araujo 1995; Peluso and Goldberg 1995; Cristina 1995).

These price differentials were further aggravated by the fact that Brazilian salaries have been on the decline. Since the inception of the Real Plan in 1994, and after discounting the effects of inflation, workers' income has lost one-third of its real purchasing power. As an example, the average monthly salary in the São Paulo metropolitan region—the wealthiest area of Brazil—declined to U.S.$375.00 in 2005, the lowest level in the past twenty years (Malavolta 2005).

In order to deal with the crisis, many members of the Brazilian middle class began paying for basic expenses with credit cards. But with high interest rates, bounced checks and unpaid credit card bills reached unprecedented numbers and personal bankruptcies soared (Peluso and Goldberg 1995). Thus, despite the relatively low rate of inflation, the Brazilian middle class was still in an economic vise so that many Brazilians continued to see emigration as an option. As one immigrant in the making put it: "Yes, the price of food in the supermarket is the same from one day to the next. But who can afford it? We earn so little!"

Aside from high prices and low wages, another powerful spur to emigration is the inability of some Brazilians to get jobs in the areas in which they were trained. During my New York study I encountered immigrant psychologists, economists, lawyers, teachers, social workers, and agronomists who simply could not find full-time jobs that paid reasonable salaries in their own fields. While far more Brazilians than ever before are attending universities and receiving degrees, the number of jobs that call for higher education has not kept pace. The nation's economic difficulties beginning in the mid-1980s and continuing today have meant that fewer jobs requiring university-level training have been created. Thus, many Brazilians with college degrees could only get positions with lower status and lower pay than their educational credentials warranted.

As a result of these conditions, some have proclaimed the "death" of the Brazilian middle class. Brazilians in New York City told me that it was now "impossible" to maintain a middle-class lifestyle in Brazil. The maelstrom of paltry wages, high prices, few good job opportunities, and continued economic uncertainty cast a pall over the lives of untold numbers of middle-class Brazilians. When they look at the future and see little hope of improving their economic situation, emigration, in effect, becomes a "what have I got to lose" option. Moreover, since most emigrants are young and single and do not need much capital to emigrate abroad—the trip is usually financed through personal savings or with loans from family or friends—emigration can be seen as a temporary, low-cost personal investment opportunity (Martes 2000).

What are the factors that make immigration to the United States so attractive? Immigrants are very precise on this point: in striking contrast to jobs in Brazil, jobs in the United States pay high enough wages to permit savings. The figure most often cited is four to one; that is, in one week in the United States immigrants can earn what it would take four weeks to earn in Brazil. The most basic enticement of immigration is the ability to earn much more money in much less time, what one immigrant called "the economy of time." Brazilians complain that even after working twenty years in Brazil, buying an apartment or a house is still out of reach of most people. In the United States the wages saved from only two or three years' labor can translate into a down payment on a home in Brazil or a nest egg to begin a small business there. And this remittance money can certainly add up. In 2006 Brazilians in the United States sent an estimated 7 billion dollars back home (Weis 2007).

Given a monthly minimum wage of U.S. $250 in Brazil (in mid-2008), it is little wonder why Brazilians find U.S. wages so appealing. It is important to emphasize, however, that for the most part, we are not dealing with minimum wage workers here. As we will see in the chapter to follow, Brazilian immigrants in New York City are generally middle class and well educated. Before coming to this country most held professional or semi-professional positions that paid good salaries by Brazilian standards. Still, in comparison to what they earn even in the most menial jobs in the United States, Brazilian salaries look feeble indeed.

At least when they first come to this country, many Brazilian immigrants are target earners, immigrants who are working to save money to pay for some specific item back home—land, an apartment, a new business. For example, the goal of many immigrants from Governador Valadares is to establish a business in Brazil that will provide them with sufficient income to meet daily expenses since their intention is to become employers rather than employees (Siqueira 2005; Duffy 2008). Several immigrants from the tiny town of Tiros in the Brazilian state of Minas Gerais are target earners who have come up with a novel way to insure that the money they earn in New Jersey arrives quickly and safely in their hometown in Brazil. Twice a year they pay the round-trip airfare from New York to Brazil of a fellow townsman who hand delivers their savings to waiting relatives. The cost of the airline ticket divided among the group of friends is much less than the

10 percent commission that remittance agencies typically charge for wiring money to Brazil. The individual who carries the small fortune in collective savings back to Brazil is chosen as the courier not only because he is a trusted friend, but because he alone among them has a green card. The green card allows him to come and go from the United States as he pleases. The other members of the group are undocumented immigrants and can not risk the trip to Brazil themselves because they might find it difficult or impossible to return to this country.

Economic motives for coming to the United States often coalesce with other motives. Another powerful draw is family reunification. For those whose relatives have been living in the United States for a decade or more and whose plans to return home are uncertain, the desire to reunite with close kin has spurred additional family members to migrate (Siqueira 2005).

Then, too, for many Brazilians, immigrating to New York has an added subtext: the experience of living in one of the world's great cities in a country that is so embedded in the Brazilian imagination. The sheer adventure and unending possibilities of the journey are also potent allures. Middle-class, urban Brazilians—the background of most immigrants in New York City—are predisposed to the lifestyles of the developed world, most particularly the United States. The appetite for "things international" helps obfuscate the harsh reality of the economic situation at home, the daily reminder that Brazil is still a developing nation. Coming to the United States and earning first-world wages—even if they are at the bottom of the local pay scale—provides middle-class Brazilians easy access to the objects that symbolize "first-world modernity" (O'Dougherty 1995:20–21).

Brazil is a land suffused with American images. By saturating the Brazilian public with representations of the good life, American-style, the Brazilian media play an inadvertent role in the emigration flow. Brazilian television and magazines transmit an unending stream of idealized messages about American patterns of consumption and behavior, about American films, American music, and American fashions, often obliquely suggesting their hegemony over the homegrown variety. It is not surprising that the opportunity to visit the source of these fanciful images is a powerful draw to aspiring immigrants.

Becoming an Immigrant

Once Brazilians decide to immigrate to the United States, the first step is figuring out how to pay for the trip itself along with the expenses of the early weeks in this country. The next step is getting a U.S. tourist visa. At first glance, financing the move looks as though it could be a problem and securing a visa seems as if it would be easy. But this is not usually the case. In fact, for most Brazilian immigrants in New York City paying for the trip was not a major obstacle. The minimum amount needed for the move to the United States is around U.S. $2,000—about U.S. $1,000 for airfare and U.S. $1,000 for initial living expenses—although most immigrants bring additional funds in case they have trouble finding work or encounter other unanticipated expenses. About two-thirds of the Brazilians in my New York study paid for the trip from their savings, or by selling a car or other personal property in Brazil, or by receiving financial help from their families in the form of loans or gifts. The remaining third financed the trip through loans, typically installment loans from travel agencies for plane tickets. But there is still another option used by an unknown but significant number of Brazilians who are not quite tourists and not quite immigrants. They come to the United States with just enough money to live on for two or three weeks and resolve that if they cannot find work in that time they will simply hop on a plane and return to Brazil, chalking up the experience as an adventure, an opportunity to see a foreign country—in this case, one that is particularly ubiquitous in the Brazilian psyche.

If financing the trip abroad is relatively easy for most Brazilian immigrants, getting a U.S. tourist visa—particularly after September 11, 2001—can be a daunting experience. To be approved for a tourist visa by American consular officers in Brazil, would-be travelers have to show that they have sufficient funds to cover their stay in the United States. More important, they must demonstrate that they have compelling reasons and resources to return to Brazil: a good job or significant property or close family ties there. In other words, they have to prove beyond a reasonable doubt that they have *no* intention of staying in the United States and seeking work, in other words, that they are not illegal immigrants in the making.

Linked to the size of one's financial resources (or lack thereof) is social class. Even prior to September 11, 2001, there was a great deal of evidence that American consular personnel were selecting for temporary stays Brazilian visitors of middle-class and elite status, while denying entry to Brazilians from more humble backgrounds (Margolis 1994, 1998b). Evidence for this comes from a scandal at the U.S. consulate in São Paulo in 1997, when a foreign service officer revealed that officials marked applications for U.S. tourist visas with codes like LP for "Looks Poor," TP for "Talks Poor," and RK for "Rich Kid." The foreign service officer said he was fired for refusing to go along with the system, arguing that the codes masked racial and ethnic discrimination (Epstein 1997; Shenon 1997, 1998).

Where children attend school can serve as a proxy for monetary resources. Because nearly all middle-class Brazilian children whose parents can afford to send them to private school do so, asking visa applicants where their children attend school is a shortcut to finding out their financial status and, hence, their qualifications for a tourist visa. In a similar vein, because poorer Brazilians have more difficulty getting tourist visas, it is said that an informal "law of three suits" (*o lei de tres ternos*) operates among American consular personnel in Brazil. If a prospective tourist has the same suit on in his passport and visa pictures and during his visit to the U.S. consulate—rather than three different suits—this is a sign that he is poor and really intends to emigrate and not just visit the United States as a tourist, and so he is denied a visa.

As a result of these constraints, during the course of my field research I met individuals in New York City who had been turned down three, four, even five times before getting a tourist visa. New York's Brazilian community is rife with tales about the pursuit of this illusive document, and it is not just Brazilians who want to immigrate to the United States who have problems, but legitimate tourists as well. Moreover, because of the tremendous demand for visas from immigrants and tourists alike, the process of getting one can consume many hours or even days if the aspiring traveler lives far from an American consular office in a major city. In fact, by 2006 it took over two months on average just to schedule an interview at the U.S. consulates in Rio de Janeiro and São Paulo (Gaspari 2006).

The long wait for a visa and the bureaucracy involved in applying for one has spawned a host of entrepreneurs who sell everything from spaces on the long snaking line in front of the U.S. consulate to visa application forms and *cafezinhos*, tiny cups of strong Brazilian coffee. On a chilly winter morning at 6:45 a.m., well over five hundred people already were standing in line in front of the modern glass building that houses the U.S. consular offices in Rio de Janeiro. One visa seeker was offered 150th place on line for U.S. $30. Promptly at 8 a.m. the consulate opened its doors and the human line began to inch forward. By 10 a.m. that day's quota of about five hundred visa applicants was filled and the consulate shut its doors. A consular employee informed the people still on line—about two hundred on a typical day—that they would have to come back at another time. After spending seven hours over two days in line, a journalist doing a magazine story on the great visa chase finally succeeded in setting foot on American territory at 9:50 a.m.—ten minutes before closing on the second day. He described his experience with evident disgust, writing that "visa applicants are made to stand for hours like mendicants in a soup line" (Mac Margolis 1994:48).

The difficulty many Brazilians encounter getting tourist visas to the United States and the boorish treatment that a few receive when they pass through immigration in this country have made headlines in Brazil. Indeed, the indignity suffered by some Brazilians upon entry into the United States has resulted in at least two lawsuits against the U.S. government. An article in the well-respected newsmagazine *The Economist* reports the unhappy experience of some Brazilian travelers (Mac Margolis 1994). One man from São Paulo—a real estate agent of considerable means who had traveled to the United States to see his compatriots play in the World Cup—was accused of carrying a false passport when he arrived at New York's Kennedy Airport and was immediately seized by U.S. immigration officials. He was held for fifteen hours, interrogated, and denied contact with his family, lawyers, or consular personnel until he "voluntarily" signed a deportation order and was put on the next plane to Brazil.

Despite forceful efforts to deny tourist visas to individuals suspected of having immigrant intentions, what most Americans do not realize is that it is actually quite easy to be transformed into an "illegal" after arriving in this country. Once getting past immigration inspection at Kennedy Airport or any other U.S. port of entry, the traveler is essentially home free because no system currently exists for keeping track of any foreign visitor, whether legitimate tourist or would-be immigrant.[3]

On to a New Land

Whether one arrives in New York, Miami, or Los Angeles—the primary ports of entry for Brazilian immigrants to the United States—the passage through immigration and customs is a nerve-wracking experience. Even though most immigrants-to-be come to the United States with valid passports and tourist visas, this does not assure automatic entrée into this country. If immigration officers suspect that an arriving passenger is not a legitimate tourist, the person is detained for questioning.

Why are some travelers suspected of being immigrants? There are several clues that a visitor actually intends to stay in this country and seek work: an inordinate amount of luggage for a short vacation stay or clothes that are inappropriate to the tourist's destination—a heavy winter coat packed for a trip to Miami, for example. Other signs of permanence are items that hint of a long-term sojourn, such as a one-year supply of birth control pills or several months' worth of prescription medications.

Having a close relative in the United States also may alert immigration authorities. The reasoning is that kin can provide a haven to newcomers, housing them and helping them find work. This is why immigrants in the making are warned by their experienced compatriots to deny, if asked, that they have family ties or even know anyone living in the United States. Finally, visitors who arrive with too little money to pay for a New York or Florida "vacation" are targeted for further questioning since this may indicate that the traveler has come not for a short-term trip but for a long-term job. As such, most Brazilians carry at least U.S. $1,000 with them—the minimum amount thought necessary to escape suspicion—even if they have to borrow the money from relatives or friends.

While most Brazilian immigrants fly to New York, Miami, or Los Angeles, more and more have been arriving in the United States via the route most often associated with undocumented immigrants; they take the long, perilous, and costly journey from Brazil to the United States through Mexico. Although in the early 1990s I met very few Brazilian immigrants in New York City who had entered the United States via Mexico, after September 11, 2001, and the increased difficulty obtaining a tourist visa, Brazilian immigrants began using this route with greater frequency, a route that will be discussed more fully in the postscript.

Suffice it to say at this point that the Mexican route is the path of last resort for Brazilian immigrants traveling to the United States. The trip through Mexico is not only more arduous and riskier, it costs three to five times as much as the more direct air route from Rio de Janeiro or São Paulo to New York or Florida. By 2005 a package that included airfare from Brazil to Mexico, transportation to the U.S. border, the assistance of a *coyote* for the actual crossing, travel to a U.S. border city, and a one-way plane ticket to the final destination could cost upwards of U.S. $10,000. Contrast this with the U.S. $1,000 to U.S. $2,000 round-trip airfare on a direct flight from Brazil to the United States paid by travelers who enter legally as tourists.

The serious drawbacks—monetary and otherwise—of coming to the United States by way of Mexico are such that only Brazilian immigrants who cannot gain entry to this country any other way even consider this route. These are individuals who have been turned down again and again for tourist visas because American consular personnel in Brazil suspect them of having immigrant intentions. They may be denied visas because they come from Minas Gerais, the Brazilian state notorious for exporting emigrants, or because they cannot demonstrate that they have adequate financial resources to make a return to Brazil likely. In either case, it is ironic that it is usually the less well-off who have to take the more costly and difficult Mexican route to achieve their goal of immigrating to this country.

When Americans think of an illegal border crosser, what immediately comes to mind is a young male from rural Mexico. This was, indeed, an accurate portrait because, until about 2000, OTMs—other than Mexicans— the term used for non-Mexicans by the U.S. Department of Homeland Security—accounted for a very small percentage of individuals who crossed the border illegally. But this is changing. Beginning in the early 1990s the number of OTMs apprehended by the Border Patrol began inching upward, and by 2005, OTMs accounted for 13 percent of those detained at the border. Apprehensions also have become much more international. Not only are OTMs now from neighboring Guatemala and El Salvador, but the Border Patrol increasingly reports the arrest of Serbians, Koreans, Turks, Indians, Chinese, Brazilians, and Poles (Yahoo News 2005).

First Things First

After arriving in the United States, Brazilians, like other immigrants, have two immediate priorities: first, finding a place to live, then finding a job. For many, the key to both is having relatives and friends in this country. Over two-thirds of the Brazilians in my New York study stayed with friends or relatives during their first days or weeks in the city or received help from them finding work. Typically, a job would be arranged for a new immigrant at a brother's or sister's or cousin's place of employment or through a friend's prior contacts in the city. These immigrant networks meant that some new arrivals were able to start work almost immediately.

New immigrants need something more than just connections to get a job. They also need a Social Security card. Here, too, immigrant networks and immigrant knowledge come into play. There is a thriving document "industry" in New York, Chicago, Los Angeles, and other cities with large immigrant populations. A counterfeit Social Security card—a "social" as

Brazilians call it—is usually purchased for about U.S. $200 early in the immigrant's sojourn in this country.

Since immigration reform legislation passed the U.S. Congress in 1986, employers have been required to ask for work papers before offering a job. But many employers will quickly hire a person once some kind of "legal" document is shown, including a Social Security card. The law does not require employers to authenticate any one of the myriad documents that the new hire may show to "prove" work eligibility. Although by 2007 the Department of Homeland Security was trying to enforce a rule requiring employers to check the validity of Social Security numbers and fire employees unable to resolve "no match" discrepancies, the rule was largely unenforced while being subject to court challenges.

Not all Brazilian immigrants could count on the assistance of relatives or friends to help them find a job; about one-quarter of those I interviewed traveled to the United States alone and knew no one when they arrived. They carried with them little more than the name and address of an inexpensive hotel or the phone number of a rooming house that caters to Brazilian immigrants. Some of these lone voyagers looked back on their first weeks in the city with a sense of wonder and pride that they had been able to endure the ordeal. They told tales of sleeping in train stations or in shoddy hotels in Times Square, of wandering city streets amid the alien cacophony of a language they did not understand, and of feeling disconnected from the teeming metropolis around them.

Whether they arrive in New York alone or accompanied by family or friends, most Brazilian immigrants find permanent quarters within a few weeks. These they share with other Brazilians, sometimes compatriots they met after coming to the city. Few Brazilians live alone; in fact, only 10 percent of those I studied in New York did so. The reasons are twofold: cost and custom. New York is an expensive city and no single item costs more than rent. As such, having friends and relatives share housing and utility bills is critical given the aim of most Brazilians—at least when they first arrive in this country—of saving as much money as quickly as possible for the return to Brazil.

Cost is not the only issue. Living alone in order to have one's private "space" is an arrangement that strikes Brazilians as rather strange. Even if they could afford to live alone, most Brazilians would choose to live with friends or relatives because in the Brazilian scheme of things living alone means being lonely. In fact, Americans and Brazilians have a very different sense of and need for privacy. Let me illustrate with a personal anecdote.

When I first went to Brazil to do summer field work I was a twenty-two-year-old graduate student. While there I lived with the family of the administrator of a sugar estate, the site of my field research. Even though the administrator's house was large and had rooms to spare, I was told that I would be sharing the small bedroom of his twelve-year-old daughter so that she could keep me company and I would not feel "too lonely" being so far from home, parents, and other relatives. My North American sense of privacy was none too pleased with this arrangement!

So both money and cultural notions of conviviality enter into the residential choices of Brazilian immigrants in New York City. This is why a married couple will take in one or two paying boarders and why a number of friends will rent a small apartment together and put up with the crowded conditions that inevitably result. Brazilians even have a word for such places. They call them *puleiros*, Portuguese for "chicken coops." Whether in an apartment or a rooming house that caters to new immigrants, a *puleiro* is a place that houses a lot of people in very cramped quarters.

Living in a *puleiro* is typically a passing phase in the life cycle of recent arrivals from Brazil. Researchers call such living arrangements "no family households," made up of single people sharing an apartment or domestic servants who live in the homes of their employers (Chavez 1989). People who reside in them are usually single migrants who plan to get a job, make money, and then return home. These households become less common as immigrants turn into settlers. Given that many Brazilian immigrants are new to this country and that most view themselves as temporary sojourners, it is not surprising that nearly 40 percent of Brazilians in my study lived in households of this type. Most of the rest live in households composed of kin. New York Brazilians are about evenly divided between those who live in simple family households that consist of a married couple with or without children or a single-parent family and those who reside in complex family households made up of varying combinations of relatives. The importance of multiple family incomes can be gauged from the fact that three-quarters of these households had two or more family wage earners.

Since the driving ambition of Brazilian immigrants, at least initially, is to save money as quickly as possible for the return home, many are reluctant to spend their hard-earned dollars setting up New York residences. After all, why put money into living accommodations when they are only temporary? Still, certain basic items are required and some Brazilians furnish their living quarters with American castoffs. Abandoned mattresses, couches, chairs, tables, electrical appliances, even clothes are sometimes retrieved from garbage cans and trash pickups. Brazilians refer to this as their "garbage decor."

The living patterns I observed among Brazilian immigrants in New York City are similar to those of other new immigrants. Immigrants of whatever nationality are often willing to live in crowded, austere settings under conditions that would never be tolerated at home. However unpleasant their current living arrangements, they are transient and worth the inconvenience, many immigrants conclude. After all, they are saving for their future and perhaps for the future of their children.

The Great Outcry

Before I continue with my portrait of Brazilians as a recent wave in the sea of transnational migrants to the United States, I must raise one issue that is central to contemporary American immigration. This is the outcry in the United States against immigrants in general, and "illegal aliens" in particular. Why do politicians and pundits denounce the immigrant "invasion," which, they claim, drains our nation of its limited social and economic resources?

The answer lies in what I call "immigrant blame," the practice of holding immigrants responsible for trends in the nation's economy that have little or nothing to do with them. To be sure, this is not a new phenomenon in our history. At least since the 1880s, immigrants have been accused of taking jobs away from native workers and lowering their wages. They have been charged with contributing to poverty, with wresting social services from more deserving citizens, and for infecting the body politic. The only thing that has changed are the nationalities of the immigrants said to be responsible for these social ills (Espenshade 1995).

Much of the rhetoric directed against immigrants is reminiscent of that which views foreigners as transgressors who must not be permitted to "dilute" what is an otherwise healthy American social order. From this vantage point immigration is deemed polluting to the physical and social environment, and immigrants themselves become metaphors for illness and disease. Then, too, some of this oratory—long a feature of xenophobic discourse—invokes threats from criminal aliens and links the rise in crime to the presence of "others" (Schneider 1998).

The immigrant blame of today can only be understood against the backdrop of changes in the American economy that have occurred over the last three and a half decades, changes that have adversely affected a broad swath of the American middle class. Immigrants as targets of blame serve as surrogates for the sense of insecurity and unease that have become a badge of contemporary American economic life. In essence, the growing inequalities in wealth and income and widespread wage deterioration have been diverted onto the backs of immigrants.

Inequality in earnings increased dramatically in the final decades of the twentieth century and the early years of the twenty-first. In 1979 the average income for the top 1 percent was thirty-three times the income of the lowest 20 percent, but by 2000 the average income of the top 1 percent was eighty-eight times that of the lowest 20 percent. Moreover, by 2004 the wealthiest 1 percent of households in the United States held more of the country's total net worth than the bottom 90 percent of households combined (Economic Policy Institute 2005; Congressional Budget Office 2006).

By the early 1970s the median wage of American men working full-time had begun its descent and men's earnings have continued to fall ever since. Then, too, while the pain of lower wages was once limited to blue-collar men who had not gone to college, the decline has now spread to college-educated white-collar men. For a number of years the decrease in average male wages was not reflected in a decline in household income because women made up the slack by taking jobs in record numbers. Household income, in fact, rose slowly until 1989. But in that year median real wages for women working full-time also began to fall. As a result, after correcting for inflation, median family income fell 7 percent from 1989 to 1993—the first such four-year stretch since World War II. Moreover, since 2000 average family incomes have fallen about 1 percent annually, all of which has meant that the incomes of American families have grown more unstable over the last generation (Mishel and Bernstein 1996; Margolis 2000; Thurow 1995; Gosselin 2004).

Jobs also have become less secure over the last two decades, intensifying the economic uncertainty of many Americans. And, the consequences of losing a job today are more troubling than in the past. As the net worth of middle income families declined, they had fewer resources to fall back on in case of job loss. Then, too, as is well known, fewer jobs now provide the health insurance and pension benefits that most middle-class Americans had come to expect.

The reasons for all of these changes are complicated and involve deregu-lation, the weakened bargaining power of employees, the shift to service sector employment, and the globalization of the economy. But the truth is that immigrants probably have done less to depress the wages of low-skilled

American workers than the millions of American women who have entered the labor force over the last three and a half decades.

The growing inequality of household income also has a demographic cause. As more single working mothers populate the lower end of the income scale, more upper-end households have two well-paid professional wage earners, making for a greater income spread (Wright 1995). And so, while new arrivals in this country logically have little to do with these complex changes, holding immigrants accountable for them has a simple and direct appeal. And it clearly makes for better politics to blame "aliens" for these painful economic shifts than to cite vague American "economic and demographic trends" as the culprits.

2

Brazilian Immigrants

A Portrait

If you were to ask an average American to describe an "illegal immigrant," he or she would doubtless say something like, "Oh, a Mexican. Probably a young guy from a poverty-stricken village in rural Mexico. Someone who's not well educated—maybe he's been through primary school, that's all. Someone who's real poor, from a very poor family that lives in a shack and maybe doesn't have enough to eat." Although many Brazilian immigrants in the United States are, in fact, undocumented—recall that just over half in my New York study were, and a decade later upwards of 70 percent lacked work papers—Brazilians bear very little resemblance to the stereotypical "illegal" of this description. Brazilian immigrants in New York City and, it appears, in other Brazilian communities around the United States are or at least were for the most part middle and lower middle class and many are well educated.

This portrait is based on data gathered on the social classes and educational levels of immigrants in New York's Brazilian community in the early 1990s. Social class is difficult to measure and in my own study I employed two means to define it. First, I looked at objective criteria to judge class affiliation—occupation of and property ownership by immigrants and their parents in Brazil and years of schooling. Then I sought self-identification; I asked Brazilian immigrants to what social class they belonged. Finally, based on all of this information, I recorded my own observations of social class membership. Table 2.1 combines and summarizes these findings.

How does the data on social class in the immigrant community compare to that in Brazil as a whole? Clearly, Brazilian immigrants in New York City represent only a portion of Brazil's social hierarchy. One index of social class—buying power—has been used in table 2.2 as an indirect gauge of the nation's class structure. A word of explanation: the scale is based on the disposable income of Brazilians, the amount and proportion of household income that remains after basic living expenses are met for food, housing, clothing, utilities, and so on. The greater the amount and percentage of income left over after these expenses are paid, the more disposable income a household is said to have, and hence the higher its social class.

Now compare the distribution of social classes nationally in Brazil (table 2.2) to the social class of Brazilian immigrants in New York City (table 2.1). In the national scale the four top classes (upper through lower middle) make up 40 percent of the Brazilian population, while in New York City these top strata make up about 90 percent of Brazilian immigrants. We see nearly the reverse of these proportions when we look at the bottom rungs of the social ladder. While the two poorest classes (working and abject poverty) account for 60 percent of the Brazilian population, only 10 percent of the immigrant population in New York is so classified. In sum, Brazilian immigrants in the city are decidedly more middle class than their compatriots back home.

Social class must be contextualized, that is, viewed from the perspective of the "sending" society. What does it mean to be middle class in Brazil? The Brazilian middle class is sometimes defined as those with *um collarinho e gravata*—a collar and tie—because a major marker of middle-class membership there is white-collar employment. In Brazil, people who work with their hands, people who do manual labor are, by definition, not middle class. This is probably why middle-class Brazilian families are far more likely than their American counterparts to employ domestic servants in their homes. It would be unthinkable for a middle-class Brazilian housewife to scrub floors or wash clothes (Margolis, Bezerra, and Fox 2001).

Almost no Brazilian immigrants in New York City were employed in occupations requiring manual labor when they lived in Brazil; nor for that matter were their parents. Close to one-quarter of the parents of immigrants in my study were business owners, strong evidence of membership in the middle or lower middle class in Brazilian society. The large proportion of professionals in this immigrant community—also nearly one-quarter of those in my New York study—is another clear indicator of middle-class status. Professionals represented in this immigrant population included journalists, engineers, agronomists, lawyers, social workers, and psychologists—all occupations associated with the middle strata of Brazilian society.

Not all of New York's Brazilians held such relatively lofty occupations back home. Lower middle-class Brazilians are also well represented in this immigrant community. Many émigrés were nurses and elementary school teachers, scandalously underpaid professions in Brazil. Others owned

Table 2.1. Social Class of Brazilian Immigrants in New York City

Social Class	Percent of Brazilian Immigrant Population
Upper middle class	11 percent
Middle and lower middle class	79 percent
Working class	10 percent

N = 100

Table 2.2. Brazil's Social Classes

Social Class	Percentage of Brazil's Population
Upper and upper middle class	6 percent
Middle and lower middle class	34 percent
Working class	34 percent
Abject poverty	26 percent

Source: adapted from Kottak (1990).

small businesses—bars and restaurants, grocery stores, auto repair shops, pharmacies—that were ravaged by their homeland's troubled economy.

Patterns of property ownership among the city's Brazilian immigrants and their parents is yet another sign of middle-class origins. In Brazil, to own a major item of property like an automobile is to be middle or lower middle class. As it turned out, over 60 percent of the immigrants in my study owned significant property in Brazil—land, a house or apartment, a car—and an even higher proportion of their parents—84 percent—owned similar property.

Data on the education of New York's Brazilian immigrant community also reflects their relatively elite class status since Brazilians based in New York have an uncommonly high level of schooling. Over three-quarters of the Brazilian immigrants in my study have at least a high school education; nearly half have some university training; and close to one-third have university degrees. To put these figures in perspective consider the fact that by the late 1990s only 32 percent of the Brazilian population had finished high school and just 12 percent of those had gone on to university. The educational level of Brazilian immigrants in New York City is impressive even by U.S. standards. After all, just 28 percent of Americans have college degrees.

Even a decade after my initial research in the early 1990s, well-educated Brazilians—including professionals—were still flocking to the city. In 2003, for example, I met young Brazilians working as waiters in Manhattan. One from Minas Gerais had completed law school in Brazil, while another had completed three years of university before coming to New York with his girlfriend. And in 2007 I became acquainted with a middle-aged woman working as a nanny in New York who had a master's degree and who had been a high school teacher in Brazil before immigrating to the United States.

The social class make-up of New York's Brazilian immigrant community also holds the key to its racial make-up. Here, too, New York's Brazilians are not representative of their nation's population because most cluster at the lighter end of the color spectrum. In my own study, 83 percent of the Brazilians I interviewed were white, 8 percent were light mulatto or mulatto, and 8 percent were black. Thus, blacks and other "people of color," to use the Brazilian phrase, account for only about 16 percent of the city's Brazilian immigrant community, a fraction of the nearly 45 percent reported in the 2000 census for Brazil as a whole (Fundação Instituto Brasileiro de Geografia e Estatística 2000).

What is the relationship between race and class in Brazil? Brazilian racial types are not randomly distributed across the nation's social classes, and people of color are overrepresented at the lower ranks of Brazilian society, underrepresented in the middle sectors, and nearly absent among the nation's tiny elite. Thus, if Brazilian immigration is mostly a middle- and lower-middle-class phenomenon—as it appears to be in New York City—it is not surprising that the immigrant population is lighter than the nation as a whole.

Nevertheless since the beginning of the new millennium there have been some shifts in the social class make-up of Brazilians coming to the United States. Unlike earlier immigrants who tended to belong to the urban middle class, some more recent émigrés have working-class roots in small towns and rural areas in Brazil. According to the Brazilian consulate's former liaison to the Brazilian immigrant community in New York, there has been a change in the socioeconomic backgrounds of Brazilians served by the New York consulate. From the mid-1980s through the 1990s, most were middle class. But from 2000 on, more were working class with at most a high school education. Once in the New York metropolitan area many of these recent arrivals take blue-collar jobs—in construction, for example—that are not so different from jobs they had in Brazil. An analysis of consular data after 2000 found that 25 percent of the Brazilian women employed as maids in the United States had been maids in Brazil, while about 10 percent of the men working as waiters had held similar positions back home (Da Costa 2004). Of course, the attraction of American jobs, however undesirable from the point of view of working conditions, is that they pay wages that are many times what similar jobs pay in Brazil.

Others have also noted that some recent immigrants come from more humble backgrounds than their trail-blazing predecessors. For example, a school psychologist in Framingham, Massachusetts points to the "different Brazils" she has encountered in her work—the urban, educated, middle-class Brazil and the rural, poorly schooled, excluded Brazil (Andreazzi 2004). Similarly, the founder of the Brazilian Women's Group in Boston notes that poorer, less educated Brazilians from interior towns began arriving there around 2000 (Souza 2004). These poorer immigrants who earlier had no access to either the information or the resources of middle-class immigrants now have both thanks to friends and relatives from the same towns in Brazil who are already established in the United States.

One case in point involves the two thousand Brazilians in Riverside, New Jersey, a town of eight thousand. Many of these new immigrants, who began arriving around 1999, come from small towns and cities in the Brazilian state of Rondonia, which up to that time had not been a source of immigrants to the United States. They have created an "immigrant niche" in Riverside as young men—most between eighteen and thirty—began arriving to work as carpenters, primarily in the once-booming home construction industry. Virtually all made their way to the United States via Mexico (Da Costa 2004; Moroz 2005a).

Most of these new immigrants from humble backgrounds do not plan to stay in the United States more than three years—just enough time to save money to buy land or a house in Brazil. One immigrant who earned up to $2,600 a month working as a carpenter returned to Rondonia with $50,000 in savings. Before coming to the United States he had an income of $200 a month making deliveries for a pharmacy. Since returning to his hometown he has bought a house, a car, several head of cattle, and he has established a supermarket there (Moroz 2005b).

But one might well ask: How do Brazilians of such modest means come to this country, especially given the current difficulty obtaining tourist visas and the high cost of entry via Mexico? One answer is that groups of some twenty to thirty Brazilians already in the United States have monthly get-togethers during which they contribute money to fund future immigrants. In a set sequence, one member of the group receives the entire fund, which is then used by a relative or friend to pay for passage to Mexico, including the services of a *coyote*, or for plane fare to the United States and the costs of obtaining a tourist visa. When the new immigrant arrives and finds work, he—and it is usually a he—begins repaying the amount he received to come to the United States. The system not only helps new immigrants pay off their debts and start saving for the return home, it also eliminates potential threats from *coyotes* to turn them over to immigration authorities if the debt is not paid in a timely manner. Finally, members of the group help newcomers to find work so that they too can begin contributing to the fund to finance other Brazilians who want to emigrate.

Still, despite the arrival of Brazilians of working-class origin after 2000, the middle classes are still dominant in New York's Brazilian population, a perception confirmed by the immigrants themselves. Most of those interviewed agreed that the vast majority of their compatriots come from the middle sectors of Brazilian society, with neither Brazil's elite nor her impoverished masses present to a very significant degree. Of course, there are wealthy Brazilians in New York, but they come as tourists not as immigrants, or they belong to a small group of executives that run the city's Brazilian banks, airlines, and corporations. Similarly, there were very few individuals in New York's immigrant community at the time of my initial study who would be considered very poor by Brazilian standards. After all, Brazil's poor—who have to struggle daily just to meet their most basic needs—are unlikely candidates for international migration.

Remittances—the money that immigrants send home—provide an important clue to social class. In Brazil, as well as in other countries, the families of immigrants that regularly rely on remittance money to meet their living expenses are usually less well-off and from a poorer sector of their own society than the families of immigrants who do not need a routine infusion of foreign cash to pay their bills. As such, remittances can be used as a yardstick of social class affiliation.

Although I found that about half of the immigrants I studied regularly or occasionally sent money home, most who frequently sent remittances were not, in fact, sending money to support their families in Brazil. Instead, they were sending it to build a nest egg for their own return home or to pay off a personal debt incurred for their trip to New York. In other words, I found very few Brazilian immigrants who provided routine financial support for their families in Brazil, further confirmation that members of Brazil's lower class are relatively few and far between in the city's Brazilian immigrant community.

Not the Huddled Masses

The social class make-up of New York's Brazilian community is not surprising since it has long been recognized that it is usually not the very poor who migrate internationally or become undocumented immigrants when they reach their destination. Thus, the class origins and high education levels of the majority of New York's Brazilian immigrants are not exceptional. Many other recent immigrants to the United States—Koreans, Indians, Peruvians, and Argentines, to name a few—have middle-class roots and their educational credentials are comparable to or even surpass those of the American population as a whole.

Why, in many cases, is it not the "huddled masses" of developing nations but their relatively well-off citizens who seek their fortunes as immigrants abroad? The relatively well-off have what is generally unavailable to the poorer elements in their own societies: the financial resources and the information needed to migrate internationally. In other words, when members of the middle strata are discouraged by economic conditions at home—when they cannot find decent jobs or are fed up with low wages or out of control inflation—they are the ones who have the discretionary income to pay for the high cost of moving abroad and the knowledge and social contacts that enable them to do so. This is particularly true of members of the urban middle class who have more ready access to the services and resources needed by potential immigrants.

Just consider what is usually involved in traveling to a distant foreign land, be it for purposes of tourism or immigration. First, one must decide where to go and then find out how to get there—airfares, flight schedules, perhaps bus or train schedules if the trip involves travel to an international airport. Then one must know how to obtain—and be able to pay for—the documents needed for the trip, usually a passport and a visa and sometimes immunization records. Knowledge about one's destination is also useful, if not essential—the rate of currency exchange, the expense of travel from foreign airport to destination city, the price and location of lodging and food, the cost of public transportation, and so on. In the case of would-be immigrants, additional information is usually needed: job opportunities at the destination abroad and the costs of living there, to cite just two obvious examples.

Another factor that clearly gives an advantage to middle-class immigrants are the bureaucratic requirements for obtaining travel documents. The comparatively affluent usually have an easier time securing them. Re-

call that when Brazilians go to the American consulate in Rio de Janeiro or
São Paulo seeking tourist visas, they must demonstrate to the satisfaction
of consular personnel that they have sufficient financial resources—a good
job or significant property—to tie them to Brazil, making it less likely that
they will stay in the United States to seek work and more likely that they
will return home. Today in Brazil the obstacles placed in the path of prospective travelers to the United States give middle-class Brazilians a distinct
advantage over their poorer compatriots, in effect making this immigrant
flow more middle class than might otherwise be the case.

Then, too, since information about economic opportunities in the destination country is crucial in the decision to migrate, immigrants tend to
go to places where they have contacts. After all, information—as well as aid
and comfort—is more likely to be available to individuals who already have
friends and relatives living in the migration locale. If, therefore, middle-
class Brazilians have family or friends who have already emigrated abroad,
they are more likely than their poorer compatriots to have access to such
information and support. In fact, for some Brazilian families, having a relative in the United States is considered "chic"; it is a sign of status. They say
they have a relative "living in America," not "working in America" (Martes
2000).

Follow the Leader

There is another intriguing dimension to social class and international migration. Research suggests that international migration is often sequenced
by social class, with middle-class immigrants paving the way for their homeland's less prosperous members (Piore 1979). It is only after information
networks that facilitate international migration have been established—
travel and remittance agencies, visa brokers, and the like—that would-be
immigrants from the lower social strata are able to follow the migratory
path abroad blazed by their nation's more affluent citizens.

Similar factors help explain the relatively recent arrival of poorer citizens
from Brazil as well as the geographical distribution of Brazilian immigrants
in various cities in the United States. Social class, educational level, place
of origin in Brazil, and place of residence in the United States all appear to
be connected. In the Boston metropolitan area Brazilians from Governador Valadares, the famed "sending community" mentioned in the previous
chapter, are more likely to be from lower-middle-class or even working-class
families than are immigrants from other parts of Brazil. Many Valadarenses

in the Boston area come from the families of farmers, schoolteachers, small shopkeepers, and military men, while immigrants from Rio de Janeiro and São Paulo are more often the children of professionals—doctors, lawyers, and businessmen (Badgley 1994). Similar enclaves of lower-middle-class and possibly working-class Valadarenses exist in Danbury, Connecticut, and Newark, New Jersey. In New York, where the vast majority of Brazilians are middle class, there are relatively few Valadarenses, most immigrants having been "big city kids"—residents of Belo Horizonte, Rio de Janeiro, or São Paulo—before immigrating to the United States.

Educational differences among Brazilian immigrants follow along similar lines. In Boston, Brazilian immigrants from Rio de Janeiro and São Paulo—like their counterparts in New York—are apt to have at least some university training, while most of those from Governador Valadares and the surrounding towns have not gone beyond high school. To summarize: Brazilian immigrants from small cities like Governador Valadares are likely to come from more modest backgrounds and have less education than those from the nation's large metropolitan centers.

How can we explain the apparent links between place of origin and socioeconomic roots in Brazil and destination city in the United States? Once again, the key seems to lie in the sequencing of migration by social class, a phenomenon that is particularly important in a relatively small community like Governador Valadares that has a long tradition of immigration to the United States. In such cases, long-term migration patterns make for strong ties between the sending community and the destination city or cities abroad. New immigrants from the community are likely to go to "familiar" U.S. cities—those where relatives or friends already have settled. This would explain, for example, the presence of several thousand Valadarenses in Framingham, Massachusetts, Danbury, Connecticut, and Pompano Beach, Florida—small cities unfamiliar to most Brazilians. And it would also account for Brazilians from the tiny community of Tiros in southern Minas Gerais who have flocked to Long Branch, New Jersey, a place not much larger than their hometown. Or consider the Brazilian enclave in Cliffside, New Jersey, just across the Hudson River from Manhattan. Most immigrants there are from Batinga, a small speck on the map in southern Bahia, a state in northeastern Brazil.

Thus, immigrants from sending communities like Governador Valadares or Tiros who establish roots in a locale abroad facilitate the migration of subsequent hometown immigrants. And this, in turn, has important implications for the social class of aspiring travelers. A fairly wide range of social classes are represented among Valadarenses in the United States, although evidence suggests that pioneer immigrants were from the middle strata of local society. As one native told me, today "all classes of Valadarenses are going to the U.S. from the rich to the poor." While perhaps that is an exaggeration, estimates suggest that about 20 percent of the town's international migrants have working-class origins, the result of a culture of out-migration that exposes citizens from diverse economic and educational backgrounds to the discourse on emigration. This discourse, coupled with the money sent back from relatives who already have immigrated to the United States, enable still more native sons and daughters to try their luck abroad. In short, in a town like Governador Valadares a culture of out-migration provides both the ideology and the material underpinnings—in the form of remittances from relatives in the United States—that make emigration possible for individuals from a range of social backgrounds.

People of modest means, then, people who in other circumstances could never hope to emigrate abroad, become international migrants with the financial help of family members or friends who migrated earlier. In this way, a pervasive culture of out-migration enhances the emigration prospects of poorer, less educated segments of the population, with the result that Valadarenses in the United States appear to have more diverse antecedents than emigrants from other regions of Brazil. Finally, this explains the presence of a working-class component in the Brazilian immigrant population of American cities where Valadarenses cluster—Boston, Newark, Danbury—but not in New York, which tends to attract urban immigrants from Brazil.

Hometowns, Stereotypes, and Social Class

Although the origins of Brazilian immigrants in my study are mixed,[1] if you were to ask the average Brazilian about his or her compatriots in the United States, the response would be something like, "Oh, those *mineiros*. They're the ones who go to the U.S. It's a wonder that there are any people left in the whole state of Minas Gerais!" In Brazil and among Brazilian populations in the United States *mineiros* are seen as quintessential migrants. Indeed, natives of the state were pioneers in the Brazilian diaspora and dominated many Brazilian communities in the United States, particularly in the 1980s during the first years of the exodus.

If *mineiros* are occasionally lauded as pioneers, they are more often vilified for a variety of real or imagined sins by their compatriots from other parts of Brazil. *Mineiros* are the butt of endless jokes, and natives of the state are the victims of unflattering stereotypes. They are said to be very provincial; they are described as unrefined rubes especially in comparison to their cosmopolitan brethren from Rio de Janeiro and São Paulo. They are also said to be crafty, exploitative, and mercenary and more than willing to take advantage of their fellow Brazilians for monetary gain.

The anti-*mineiro* sentiment expressed in New York's Brazilian immigrant community likely is rooted in geographical and rural-urban distinctions brought from home. What we are seeing here is a revamping and updating of the traditional discourse of urban Brazilians, especially those from major metropolitan areas such as Rio de Janeiro and São Paulo, who have a long tradition of maligning people from the interior of their country, calling them unlettered *caboclos*, *caipiras*, or *sertanejos* (hillbillies, hicks, or backwoodsmen).

Let me provide a few examples of some similar, albeit class-based stereotypes current among Brazilians in the United States. Some members of the Brazilian elite[2] in New York refer to West 46th Street, "Little Brazil"—the midtown Manhattan street with restaurants and businesses catering to Brazilian immigrants and tourists alike—as the *baixada*, a miserable swampy, impoverished, crime-ridden zone just outside the city of Rio de Janeiro. One member of the elite who lives in a wealthy suburb north of the city said that although she would like to read *Veja*, the Brazilian newsmagazine, she would not go to the *baixada* to buy a copy. Similarly, the owner of an upscale Brazilian restaurant located several blocks from Little Brazil said, "It's fine if people want to go there but we attract a better class of people." Calling Little Brazil by the name of what is arguably the most horrific place in Brazil reveals the disdain that some of New York's elite Brazilians evince toward their immigrant compatriots. It also validates the social chasm that exists between the elite and Little Brazil's merchants, who, although successful in business, generally come from fairly modest backgrounds in Brazil.

A similar story is told in the Brazilian community in Boston. An American nun was talking with an employee of the Brazilian consulate in that city. When she heard that the consular employee lived in Brighton, she asked, "Do you know many Brazilians there?" The woman responded, "Here, my dear, we don't have Brazilians; we only have illiterates." Later when this woman introduced the American nun to her friend, she presented her as a Brazilian. "But I'm not Brazilian," the nun said. The woman was surprised. "You're not Brazilian? Then how did you learn to speak such excellent Portuguese?" The nun responded, "I learned it from the illiterates in northeastern Brazil" (Martes 1995).

Whatever the origin of these regional and socioeconomic stereotypes, their existence reminds us that immigrant communities should not be blithely depicted as harmonious ethnic groups, nor should we assume a romanticized conception of ethnic solidarity that is often portrayed in the literature. In other words, we should not ignore differences in origin, social class, education, race, time of arrival in the United States, and legal status, variants that may divide rather than unite immigrant communities (Pessar 1995; Resende 2005).

For example, the varying times of arrival in the United States of immigrants from the same country can lead to rancorous divisions within an immigrant community. I found this to be true among Brazilians in New York City, and research among other immigrant populations—Brazilians in Boston, Central Americans in Washington, D.C., and Salvadorans on Long Island—confirms it (Martes 2000; Pessar 1995; Mahler 1995). Newly arrived, unseasoned immigrants are sometimes exploited, or at least ignored, by their compatriots who migrated earlier. For example, I was told that old-timers in New York's Brazilian immigrant community do not help newcomers with advice about jobs and housing, "they just pass along the suffering." Some immigrants also directed their ire at well-established Brazilians who, having lived in New York for decades, now own prosperous businesses in the city. They are loathe, claim their critics, to assist "greenhorn" Brazilians, seeing them as a potential source of future competition. Further evidence of the split between old and new immigrants comes from reports that more experienced immigrants sometimes demand that their newly arrived countrymen and women pay them "finder's fees" for telling them about available jobs (Martes 2000; Pessar 1995).

These examples suggest that the conditions that are often taken for granted among immigrant groups—ethnic solidarity and strong social support networks—sometimes do not exist or exist only in attenuated form in certain immigrant communities. Thus, we should not take ethnic unity among immigrant populations as a given, but rather consider the factors that either enhance or inhibit its development.

Among the factors that may inhibit a sense of solidarity within an immigrant community are the burdensome financial demands placed on new immigrants. An anthropologist who studied Hispanic immigrants points out the tremendous pressure they are under to earn a lot of money in a short period of time. They not only have to meet daily expenses, but they may also have to pay off debts incurred for their travel to the United States, send remittances to relatives, and save money for their own return home. Such pressures "lead to the suspension of many social ties that conditioned life before migration. These immigrants thus come to the United States expecting to find their old community solidarity, but encounter a competitive, aggressive sub-culture instead" (Mahler 1995:30). Then, too, in cases where immigrant communities are divided along class lines, class interests often overpower ethnic solidarity. "Ethnicity becomes relevant and significant when class interests coincide," concludes a researcher who studied Korean immigrants in this country (Yoon 1991:317).

Vital Statistics

Aside from social class, race, education, and hometown origin, what else characterizes this immigration stream? While I only have detailed data on Brazilian immigrants in New York City, there is reason to believe that their profile, except where specifically noted, is similar to those in other parts of the United States. Today, for example, there are only slightly more men than women in New York's Brazilian community, although evidence suggests that during the first years of immigration in the mid-1980s men accounted for perhaps 70 percent of the immigrant population. A similar imbalance in the ratio of men to women also existed at the start of this migration surge in Boston and other cities with Brazilian immigrant enclaves (Martes 2000).

While today the sex ratio in New York is about even, women do outnumber men in one age cohort: those over forty. This is best explained by one of the following scenarios. Young Brazilian immigrants often invite their mothers to visit them in New York and many of these women, especially those who are widowed, separated, or divorced and who may have planned to stay in the United States only a month or two, keep delaying the return home. Other women come to New York to care for their grandchildren for a time while the parents are working; then they simply stay on. Still others do go back to Brazil only to return to New York after a few months. While they are in the city many of these women take an occasional job babysitting or cleaning houses, which eventually turns into more permanent work—most often some form of domestic service—and become immigrants themselves.

The Brazilian population in New York City was quite young during the first phase of my research. Nearly 40 percent of the Brazilians I studied were under thirty years old, while a slightly higher percentage were between thirty and forty; only 5 percent were over fifty. At the time of my original study children comprised a relatively small segment of New York's Brazilian immigrant population, but their numbers are increasing as this immigrant stream ages. The greater presence of children, in turn, is related to the growing number of married immigrants. Sixty percent of the immigrants in my research sample in the early 1990s were single when they came to New York, about 25 percent were married, and the rest were separated, divorced, or widowed, but many immigrants married after coming to the United States.

Most married couples live together in New York. The pattern of one spouse remaining behind in the country of origin while the other seeks his or her fortune abroad and sends money home is uncommon among Brazilian immigrants in the city. But it is somewhat more frequent among immigrants from Governador Valadares. Perhaps one-third of the small community of Valadarenses in New York are single or divorced women with children being cared for by relatives in Brazil or men who send remittances to their spouses and/or children back home. These same arrangements are also more prevalent in some other Brazilian enclaves in the United States, especially those with many Valadarenses or other small emigrant-sending communities in Brazil.

This pattern is likely related to the socioeconomic class and financial resources of immigrants and their families prior to their departure from Brazil. That is, if financially able, married couples usually travel to the United States together, but the families of those who have difficulty paying for the trip stay behind in Brazil. As a result, single and divorced mothers with children in the care of relatives in Brazil and married men with families there were described to me in similar terms; they were called "money machines" and the "bankers" for their relatives back home.

Among Family

When they arrive in New York even unmarried immigrants or those whose spouses and children stayed in Brazil may have relatives in the city. Indeed, the more recent arrivals have come to the United States via chain migration, a process through which new immigrants are brought to the host country with the help—financial and otherwise—of relatives or friends who are already there. One immigrant is followed by others, with additional immigrants bringing with them ties of kinship and friendship to still more people back home. Those in the sending community, in turn, have ever expanding networks in the destination locale. Migrant streams become self-perpetuating after they start to flow, because migration becomes easier as each new immigrant lessens the cost of later migration for a network of relatives and friends. And with reduced costs, still more people are enticed to try their luck abroad, creating still more links between sending and receiving communities (Massey 1988).

Among the Brazilians I studied, the general rule was that the longer immigrants had been in New York the more relatives they had helped bring to the city. Some had sponsored dozens of family members—siblings, cousins, parents, nieces, nephews, even in-laws—while others had also aided close friends. One Brazilian who had lived in New York for over a decade told me that he had helped so many family members come to the city that he had lost count. Another longtime resident had sponsored her four siblings, their spouses, and innumerable nieces and nephews.

Chain migration typically involves more than just assistance in funding the trip. There are many advantages to having a network of family and friends in an unfamiliar city such as New York. Already settled relatives can reduce the cost of the newcomer's first days or weeks by providing a place to stay and giving advice on transportation and other aspects of city living. They can help locate work through personal contacts or knowledge of the job market. And when newly arrived Brazilian immigrants speak of their *saudades*, their deep longing for their native land, there is no one like a close relative to soothe the sting of loneliness during their early days in an alien metropolis. Thus, kin can diminish the costs of migration, both material and emotional, in many ways.

This, then, is a broadly painted portrait of Brazilian immigrants in New York City. They are mostly middle class and fairly well educated and many come from large cities in Brazil. Nevertheless, as we will see in the chapter to follow, the niche Brazilian immigrants occupy in the city's labor market reflects neither their antecedents nor their abilities. Because they are new immigrants, many of whom lack English skills and work papers, they find themselves on the lowest rung of New York's employment ladder.

Working New York

Brazilian immigrants clean houses, offices, and hotel rooms, take care of kids, and walk dogs. They drive radio cabs and limousines. They dance in go-go bars and shine shoes and they sell books and food on the city's sidewalks. They bus tables, wash dishes, and deliver pizzas. They paint and renovate apartments and houses and do landscaping in the suburbs. Since Brazilians are in the United States to earn money, they take whatever jobs are available to newcomers in this country who have little knowledge of English and no work papers. In short, despite the educational level of many Brazilian immigrants, language and legal status determine their niche in the labor market.

Before exploring the actual work that Brazilian immigrants do, it is important to understand where the labor of Brazilians and other recent immigrants in the city fits into New York's complex job market. To do that we must look beyond the city and adopt a global perspective on immigration. Evidence suggests that U.S. employers seeking low-cost labor either find it in low-wage countries abroad—the path taken by many American manufacturing firms—or they use cheap imported labor in the form of immigrant workers. Unlike manufacturers, businesses in the service sector of the economy have to follow the latter course because services require local labor—restaurants need busboys and dishwashers, motels need chambermaids, and companies that clean offices need a janitorial staff. Since these businesses obviously cannot export themselves, many come to rely on low-cost imported labor.

The need for such labor is especially acute in cities like New York, Washington, Miami, and Los Angeles that have major service industries (Repak 1995). Still, a debate exists about what is causing the rise in demand for immigrant workers in these and other cities. Some researchers argue that the number of low-wage service jobs has increased significantly in recent years; the more jobs, the greater the demand for workers to fill them (Sassen-Koob 1986). Others suggest immigrants have found this type of employment, not because there are more jobs per se, but because service sector jobs are being abandoned by many who traditionally held them (Waldinger 1989, 1996).

Each side of the debate can be outlined as follows. In certain cities like New York, jobs in the low-wage service sector are burgeoning because of the expanded presence of high-income individuals there. The needs of the wealthy and the upper middle class, the top 20 percent of the population with considerable discretionary income, have fueled the growth of personal service jobs such as live-in nannies and other domestic servants, dog walkers, drivers, restaurant workers, caterers, beauticians, manicurists, and the like. These high-income earners are upper level managers and professionals employed in New York's banking, investment, trading, communications, retail, and advertising industries. These same industries also create their own market for low-wage, low-skill jobs—for office cleaners, stock clerks, and messengers.

In short, low-wage workers are required to service the household needs and elaborate consumption patterns of an expanding high-income elite. As such, the growth of work in services leads to a more bifurcated job structure. On one side is the demand for workers willing to take low-paying, low-status, unstable jobs that generally appeal only to those with few or no alternatives, like new immigrants. On the other, there is the demand for highly skilled and highly paid executives, managers, and professionals who inhabit the upper reaches of the city's corporate structure.

Other researchers argue, however, that it is changes in the labor supply that explain the increased demand for immigrant workers. Here the reasoning is that as the proportion of white workers has declined in cities such as New York, Boston, Chicago, and Los Angeles, a "vacancy chain" has been set in motion that allows nonwhites and some immigrants to move up the job ladder (Waldinger 1989:221). Immigrants, at least initially, are replacement labor. Over time they carve out their own occupational niches, developing channels of labor market information, support, and recruitment.

Why Immigrants?

Whatever its specific cause, a demand exists for cheap immigrant labor in New York and other cities with burgeoning service sectors. The crucial question is: Why immigrants? This has become a highly contentious issue in recent years with a few researchers and many politicians and political pundits, such as CNN's Lou Dobbs, asserting that immigrants, particularly undocumented ones, are taking jobs that would otherwise be filled by citizens, or at least by legal residents of this country (Brimelow 1995; Briggs and Moore 1994). Is this true? Are newcomers *really* taking jobs that would be held by Americans, including members of native-born minority groups?

In order to answer this question, we must look at the nature of the low-wage service sector jobs that employ new immigrants. One of the key attributes of these jobs is the ease with which workers holding them are replaced. As a result, employers have scant interest in maintaining a stable labor force and this, in turn, makes for short-term jobs with little or no security and meager hope of advancement. High labor turnover also reflects the premium that many service sector employers place on a flexible work force; one that expands and contracts as the need warrants. Flexibility is an integral part of many low-wage service jobs because they are not unionized. This allows a work environment in which employers can control workers in direct and, at times, arbitrary ways. Workers in such jobs can be dismissed with little cause or their work shifts can be changed without notice.

Then, of course, there is the low rate of pay and the absence of fringe benefits that characterize this work. Many service sector jobs pay the minimum wage or somewhat more; in others a worker's income varies a good deal because it depends largely on tips. Moreover, low-wage service jobs are often done under difficult working conditions; they may involve considerable physical labor and work at odd hours, such as nights and weekends.

Finally, some substantial but unknown portion of low-wage service jobs belongs to the informal economy. Jobs in the informal economy are unregulated in terms of working conditions, wage and hour laws, and taxes withheld. As such, it comes as no surprise that informal sector jobs are the ones *least* likely to demand work papers or otherwise require immigrants to document their legal status.

Restaurant work illustrates most of the conditions that characterize low-wage service employment. Jobs washing dishes in steamy kitchens and busing heavy loads of dirty dishes—work typically done by new immigrants—require little English and minimal skill, and the workers doing them are easily replaced. Employees are often called on to work nights and weekends, and full-service restaurants usually have two shifts of workers whose numbers vary according to the time of day and the season of the year. Seasonal layoffs are not uncommon. Turnover in these jobs is generally high, as low wages, lack of benefits, and sometimes grueling working conditions sap employee morale. A study done in 2005 of the New York restaurant industry found that most restaurant workers in the city—at least 36 percent of whom were undocumented immigrants—earned less than $20,000 a year and that very few of these jobs provided benefits or opportunities for advancement. Nearly 75 percent of restaurant employees in New York City, for example, have no health insurance (Greenhouse 2005; Fickenscher 2005).

All of this points to one stark fact: low-wage service jobs are undesirable by almost any standard. They are jobs that people with other employment options simply reject. So the question then becomes: Who would *want* such jobs? Not Americans, argue some researchers, including those from native disadvantaged groups (Briggs and Moore 1994; Fix and Passel 1994; Lowenstein 2006). New immigrants, however, especially those without papers, have few alternatives and thus become "ideal" workers from the vantage point of employers. The truth is that immigrants—and again, most particularly undocumented immigrants—have less power than native-born workers. Immigrants are less likely to challenge poor working conditions, long hours at substandard wages, and abrupt firings. They are much more likely than American workers "to go along to get along." After all, what are their options? Other low-wage jobs under similarly difficult conditions?

This is why new immigrants—with or without work papers—are welcomed with open arms by many low-wage employers, be they the owners of chic Manhattan restaurants looking for dishwashers or harried career women in need of nannies to care for their children or immigrant entrepreneurs seeking seamstresses for their sweatshops. Take certain jobs in domestic service as an example. A long-term nanny in New York City had this to say about her pivotal role: "We could close down the city. . . . If there's a garbage strike, the trash just lies there. If there's a postal strike, the mail doesn't get delivered. But if the nannies were to strike it would be different. You can't just leave a baby around until there's someone ready to take care of it" (quoted in Cheever 1995:87).

Since recent immigrants constitute a large, pliant labor force with few employment opportunities, their absence would either mean higher labor costs or low-wage service jobs that went begging. For this reason, it is difficult to deny the assertion that a slice of the American economy is "hooked on" undocumented immigrant labor. And, in fact, undocumented immigrants comprise up to 5 percent of the U.S. labor force (Passel, Capps, and Fix 2004).

Does the presence of cheap, docile immigrant labor adversely affect native workers as is commonly thought? Most economists agree that in the short run immigrants who work for cheap wages can depress pay in low-skilled jobs. Nevertheless, there is little evidence that immigrants have a sizeable or long-term effect on wage structure. For example, the Mariel boatlift, which saw an influx of 125,000 unskilled workers in the city of Miami—7 percent of the total labor force—had no demonstrable effect on the unemployment rate or wage levels of unskilled non-Hispanic workers there. In short, wage growth and decline for both skilled and unskilled jobs appear to be unrelated to immigration. New immigrants, in fact, appear to have a negative effect on the labor market opportunities of only one group: immigrants who immediately preceded them (Wright 1995; Butcher and Card 1991; Fix and Passel 1994).

The one area in which new immigrants can have a negative impact on Americans, especially native minority groups, is in hiring. Evidence suggests that for some jobs immigrant employment networks are the key to new hires, who are likely to come from within the immigrant community itself. While networks benefit employers by supplying them with a stable pool of inexpensive labor and lowering recruitment and training costs, they also tend to shut out members of American minority groups from the hiring process (Waldinger 1993).

We can see how this works in one low-wage Brazilian immigrant employment enclave: shoeshining. In the early 1990s Brazilians had a near monopoly on jobs shining shoes in shoe repair shops and kiosks around Manhattan. In fact, all of the Brazilian shoeshiners in my study found their jobs through word of mouth in the Brazilian community. While shining shoes does not require much training, new immigrants need some familiarity with the techniques and products of the trade; this they get from fellow Brazilians the first day on the job. It is obvious, then, why such immigrant networks are useful to employers; they can reduce the cost of hiring and training new workers to almost nothing.

Hard at Work

If low-wage service sector jobs are so undesirable, why do Brazilians or other recent immigrants even *want* them? The answer is unambiguous: the key attraction of such jobs is that they pay considerably more money than the newcomers were earning back home. For example, by 2005 Brazilian immigrants living in New York and New England were earning a minimum of $300 a week, with a majority earning between $500 and $1,000 weekly (Siqueira 2005). Some domestic servants as well as the few Brazilians in the city working in renovation and construction make $12 to $15 an hour;

although much less than union scale for construction jobs, the rate is still an impressive sum by Brazilian standards.

To understand just how attractive U.S. wages are even in low-paying jobs, simply compare them to the earnings of Brazilian immigrants before they left home. Consider the fact that, as noted earlier, by 2005 the average *monthly* salary in the São Paulo metropolitan area—the wealthiest region of Brazil—had declined to U.S. $375.00, the lowest level in two decades, and that per capita income for the nation as a whole was less than one-tenth that of the United States (Malavolta 2005). As a result, even though many of the new immigrants were employed in Brazil in professional or semi-professional positions that paid good salaries by local standards, they are meager in comparison to what they earn in the United States, even in the type of low-wage service jobs discussed above.

A few examples of what Brazilians were earning before and after they came to the United States illustrate this point. One woman whose salary had been only U.S. $200 a month as the head nurse in a big city hospital in Brazil was making nearly five times as much in the early 1990s as a babysitter in New York, while another immigrant who was paid U.S. $500 a month as a mechanical engineer in Brazil earned U.S. $400 a week working as a private chauffeur in New York. The head of housekeeping at a swank residential hotel in Rio de Janeiro was paid a mere U.S. $430 a month for a six-day work week, a fraction of what she earned cleaning apartments in Manhattan. In dozens of similar examples given to me by Brazilian immigrants in the city, differences in the rates of pay were typically four to one; one month's earnings in Brazil were the equivalent of one week's pay in the United States. And this same four to one ratio has been reported for other parts of the United States with resident Brazilian populations (Sales 2007).

While low-wage jobs in the United States seem lucrative to those accustomed to Brazilian pay scales, do recent immigrants even receive the minimum wage?[1] What about all the news accounts that suggest that new immigrants, especially those without work papers, often receive substandard wages? Evidence suggests that relatively few undocumented immigrants earn less than the legal minimum wage, with two major exceptions: agriculture and the apparel industry—neither of which employ Brazilians. I encountered no Brazilians, for example, working anything like the exhausting sixty-hour-a-week regime for only $600 to $800 a month that has been reported for undocumented Chinese immigrants in the garment industry in New York City (Kwong 1994).

Even if employers of low-wage service workers usually pay the minimum wage or somewhat more, many still benefit financially because they often pay "off the books." By skirting the law and failing to pay Social Security taxes, unemployment compensation, and other fringe benefits, employers can save thousands of dollars annually.

Just who works off the books? The legal status of the worker seems to be less important than the type of job held. Certain jobs, like those in domestic service and shoeshining, usually are part of the informal economy, that is, they are "off the books," while restaurant work ordinarily is not. Yet, it is also true that undocumented Brazilians are more likely than legal immigrants to work as maids, babysitters, shoeshiners, street vendors, and in other typical off-the-books employment. Legal immigrants have green cards, a document issued by the U.S. Department of Homeland Security that gives the noncitizen the right to paid employment. Even Brazilians working on the books rarely receive benefits of any kind. "Health insurance? What's that?" joked one Brazilian immigrant with a slightly bitter edge in her voice. The failure to pay overtime and the absence of worker's compensation for those injured on the job are particular sources of irritation in the immigrant community.

Conventional wisdom has it that while immigrants neither earn much nor receive any benefits while working under often arduous conditions, their situation is not as unfair as it seems because they do not pay income or Social Security taxes. This is part of the image—now very much in vogue—of the immigrant as "freeloader" who receives more than she or he contributes to American society. While I lack data on this for Brazilian immigrants, research on other immigrant groups questions this assumption. For example, one study of undocumented Mexican women found that nearly three-quarters of them worked "on the books" and had both Social Security and income taxes withheld from their wages; only those employed as domestic servants and paid in cash did not (Simon and DeLey 1986). Another study of undocumented immigrants from several countries living in the New York area came up with similar findings. Nearly all of the immigrants had paid Social Security taxes and about 70 percent had also paid state and federal income taxes (Papademetriou and DiMarzio 1986). An interesting question in this regard and one that is rarely asked in the discussions about "freeloaders" is this: What happens to all of the money that immigrants pay into Social Security but never collect because they leave the country before retirement? One estimate suggests that 7 million undocumented immigrants in the United States provide the Social Security system with a subsidy of as much as $7 *billion* annually through payroll taxes withheld from their wages, money they will not receive when they retire (Porter 2005a).

Making Ends Meet

How do immigrants in low-wage jobs manage to make ends meet in an expensive city like New York and still save money for the return home? The answer is twofold: hard work and shared expenses. By working long hours, often nights and weekends, Brazilian immigrants are able to earn what they regard as good money. For example, drivers of radio call cars willing to work twelve-hour shifts six days a week can take home $600, a considerable sum by Brazilian standards. Or, by working many hours and cleaning at least two apartments a day, an immigrant can earn as much as $800 a week, although $500 to $600 is more typical. The income of busboys also can reach $500 a week for those willing to put in the hours, and the few Brazilians who work as waiters earn still more. The majority of Brazilians in New York City probably earn somewhere between $2,000 and $2,500 a month, but the combined income of couples is often much higher. For example, a married couple working together can net $3,500 to $4,000 a month cleaning at least two apartments or houses a day since taxes and Social Security are rarely withheld for domestic jobs.

Some Brazilian immigrants make up for their low wages by working two jobs, including a fair number with two full-time jobs. Almost a quarter of the immigrants I studied were holding more than one job at the time I interviewed them. Restaurants are the most common source of second jobs because their work hours are usually flexible and often involve nights and weekends. Immigrants with two jobs led truly frantic lives doing little but traveling back and forth to work and home again to catch a few hours of sleep.

Chico, a former high school teacher in Rio de Janeiro, was employed in two full-time jobs six days a week. He awoke at 6:30 a.m. and took the subway from Queens to Manhattan to begin work by 7:15 at a shoeshine shop near Penn Station. He shined shoes for the next eleven hours and then caught the subway to Greenwich Village, where he began his evening shift as a dishwasher in a restaurant. He worked almost nonstop in the restaurant's kitchen until 11:00 p.m. and then, exhausted, he boarded the subway back to Queens. On Sunday, his one day off, he slept, did the laundry, and wrote letters to his family in Brazil.

Aside from hard work, Brazilian immigrants also try to make ends meet and still save money by minimizing expenses, which they do in several ways. Since rent is their most costly budget item, the vast majority share living quarters with friends or relatives, dividing not only the cost of rent but also utilities and telephone. Then, too, it is not uncommon for married couples to take in boarders to help defray expenses. Brazilian immigrants also spend as little as possible on household items. Since, at least initially, most view their stay in New York as temporary, they don't put much money into furniture or household goods that they will not be able to take home with them to Brazil.

Frugality also plays a role in the personal attire of some New York Brazilians who are unwilling, especially at first, to spend money on winter clothes. Their reasoning is the same: Why waste hard-earned dollars on heavy coats, sweaters, and boots when they will soon be escaping New York's frosty clime and heading back to their sunny homeland?[2] Yet winter in the city requires proper dress, if only a warm coat, a scarf, and gloves. A few Brazilian immigrants have a cost-free solution to this apparel dilemma; they pick up an assortment of donated used clothing from a social service agency in Queens that otherwise caters to the city's needy and homeless.

Brazilian immigrants also are careful about what they spend on entertainment, not a difficult issue given the long hours they work and the little time most have for leisure activities anyway. This is particularly true during the first months in New York when many new immigrants turn into fanatical money-making machines whose entire existence is caught up in saving for the return home. "Leisure is very costly here," they say, because it takes time from working, and less work means less money. And, in an expensive city like New York, going to movies, concerts, bars, and restaurants can swallow up a lot of dollars that otherwise might end up in a savings account.

Time for a Change

Given the low pay and dead-end nature of the work most Brazilian immigrants do, it is no surprise that they are not tied to their jobs and change them often. This was a source of some frustration during my research when I went to a restaurant or a shoe repair shop to locate Brazilians I had interviewed in the past only to find that my former interviewees had vanished and other Brazilians were working in their places. Immigrants continually hop from job to job as they look for better wages, hours, and working conditions. For example, over the eight months I tracked the dizzying career path of one Brazilian immigrant, he was a part-time handyman, street vendor, shoeshiner, homecare attendant, bakery store clerk, and radio call car driver. My own experience confirmed the observation of another immigrant, who suggested that if I were to wait one year and then return to the place of work of all the Brazilians who had been part of my original study, I would be lucky to encounter even one or two of them since nearly all would have moved on to different jobs.

For immigrants to change jobs so often, other jobs must be available, which raises the ever controversial issue of the employment of undocumented immigrants. Recall that about half of the Brazilians in my original study were undocumented and that by 2005 up to 70 percent of Brazilians in the greater New York metropolitan area lacked work papers. In 1986 the U.S. Congress passed the Immigration Reform and Control Act known as IRCA, the primary aim of which was to stem the flow of undocumented immigrants entering the United States by making it unlawful for employers to hire them.[3] The rationale behind this legislation was that by subjecting employers to fines of up to $2,000 for hiring undocumented workers—those without proper papers—jobs for such workers would dry up. Then, without the magnet of jobs, undocumented immigrants would return to their native lands and others would be discouraged from coming to this country.

Things did not turn out that way. Despite some initial success, it is generally agreed that IRCA cut the flow of undocumented immigrants far less than expected. In fact, over the long run IRCA did nothing to stem the tide of undocumented immigration to the United States. When the law was passed in 1986 there were an estimated 4 million immigrants without the legal right to work in this country, but by 2008 there were an estimated 12 million (Bean, Edmonston, and Passel 1990; Porter 2005b; Suro 2006; *New York Times* 2008).

One reason for this failure is clear. While there were somewhat fewer jobs for undocumented workers than before IRCA was passed, the economic conditions back home that propelled Brazilians and other immigrants to come to this country in the first place remained largely unchanged. As a result, there is no evidence that immigrants became so discouraged by the effects of IRCA that they simply gave up and went home. In one study of the law's impact, not a single immigrant questioned knew anyone who had left the United States because IRCA had made it harder to get a job (Repak 1995).

My own and similar research suggests that the recession of the early

1990s and the subsequent loss of low-wage service jobs had a greater impact on the employment of Brazilians and other immigrants than IRCA's threat of sanctions against employers who hire undocumented workers (Repak 1995). While some employers do indeed require workers to show firm proof that they are "legal," most simply ask to see a Social Security card. This is easy enough to arrange since counterfeit Social Security and green cards can be bought for $100 to $200 in one of the thriving markets for bogus documents that exist in New York and other U.S. cities with large immigrant populations (Porter 2005b).

In general, IRCA's sanctions have never been seriously enforced. After September 11, 2001, the newly established Department of Homeland Security initially focused on terrorism and nearly stopped policing workplaces for routine violations. To wit, there were only 450 undocumented immigrant workplace arrests in 2003, down from 14,000 in 1998. Moreover, while over 1,000 employers were fined in 1992 for illegal labor violations, that number had plummeted to a piddling 78 employers by 2001 (Porter 2005b; Ketcham 2006). Still, with the outcry against "illegal aliens" in the U.S. Congress, enforcement increased and by 2007 Immigration and Customs Enforcement (ICE), a division of the Department of Homeland Security, had arrested more than 35,000 undocumented workers (Preston 2008a).

Nevertheless, employers have continued to hire undocumented immigrants not only because employer sanctions have not been aggressively enforced, but because in a number of areas the demand for cheap labor is not being met by native workers or even by legal immigrants. Then, too, for some employers the financial benefits of hiring off-the-book workers outweigh the cost of possible sanctions (Mahler 1995). In other words, some employers have been so desperate for low-wage workers that it matters little whether those hired are documented or not.

Employers sometimes collude with undocumented workers in skirting the law by telling them where they can buy counterfeit work papers and Social Security cards so that they can be hired "legally." This is particularly true in those industries that historically have relied on cheap illegal immigrant labor. If low labor costs are foremost, then complying with the law is relatively simple: a document, any document, will do since employers are under no legal obligation to check the validity of the "work papers" shown to them.[4]

Just What Do They Do?

Legal or otherwise, Brazilian immigrants get jobs. They can usually find work cleaning apartments, caring for children, shining shoes, washing dishes, and busing tables with little more than a reference from a friend or relative. Since coming to the United States, the 100 Brazilians in my study had been employed in a total of 325 jobs, for an average of 3.25 jobs apiece.

Women had worked in fewer job categories than men largely because the great majority of immigrant women in New York had been employed at one time or another in a single job classification—domestic service. In fact, four out of five Brazilian women in my study had worked as live-in housekeepers, day maids, nannies, and/or babysitters. No single job category employed nearly as high a proportion of men. The only one that came close was restaurant work, which comprised 30 percent of total male employment.

But both men and women had worked in a wider range of jobs than I had expected, some of which, like school teaching, banking, and retail sales, are not usually associated with immigrants. This reflects the fact that while my study population was mostly composed of new immigrants, more than 10 percent had lived in New York for a decade or more. As relative "old-timers," some had ascended the employment ladder and no longer held jobs typical of recent immigrants. The major job categories in which Brazilian immigrants are employed are profiled below.

Keeping House in New York

Over the last three decades the demand for household workers has expanded dramatically in the greater New York area and elsewhere in the United States. The transformation of the middle-class housewife-mother into a full-time salaried employee has meant that housework and, in some cases, child care have been given over to paid domestics (Margolis 2000). The nature of domestic service also has changed in recent years. Today household servants are more likely to come in to clean once or twice a week or to work for companies such as Merry Maids than to be employed full-time by a single family (Johnston 1995). Despite these changes, the long American tradition of the immigrant domestic continues. Although New York is not yet like Los Angeles or San Diego, cities in which domestic work has become an occupation done almost exclusively by undocumented female labor, housecleaning and child care are by far the most important sources of employment for undocumented Brazilian women.

We tend to think of domestic service as an all-female occupation and women do indeed dominate it among Brazilian immigrants in New York City, but a few Brazilian men also are employed in this job category. About 13 percent of the male immigrants I interviewed had done domestic work at some point since coming to this country. They cleaned houses or worked as butlers, valets, or chauffeurs. Some of these men were part of a married pair jointly employed as domestics in a single household. Hired by affluent families in the New York metropolitan area, such couples usually lived in the homes of their employers. The woman was typically charged with cooking, cleaning, and child care, while her husband served as the family butler, gardener, and/or chauffeur.

Domestic work done by immigrant women encompasses two distinct jobs: live-in housekeeper and day maid. Live-in domestic servants reside and work in the homes of their employees, while day maids or housecleaners have their own residences and typically clean a number of apartments on a rotating schedule. Living-in has both major benefits and serious costs. Live-in jobs are particularly well suited to immigrants who have just arrived in the United States. Such employment not only provides a cost-free place to live with no commuting expenses, but the new immigrant does not have to worry about arranging for telephone or utilities or learning how to use public transportation. And, with living expenses held to a minimum, newcomers are able to save quite a lot of money in a short period of time. Even at the lower end of the pay scale in New York, a frugal live-in can put away $2,000 to $2,500 a month. For all these reasons, live-in housekeeping is often the first job a woman has when she comes to the city. Half of the Brazilian women I interviewed had worked as live-ins, most soon after they arrived in this country.

The major disadvantage of these positions is their vast potential for exploitation. Living-in is seldom an eight-hour-a-day job; some families expect live-ins to be at their beck and call at all times except on their days off. As such, live-ins may lack lives of their own and become isolated from the rest of the immigrant community. One Brazilian told me how six days a week her life was a continual maelstrom of cooking, cleaning, doing the laundry, and caring for a rambunctious three-year old. The live-in's job is never done because her home and place of work are the same.

Despite its drawbacks, several Brazilian women consider the ordeal of life as a live-in a price worth paying because it can provide a rare opportunity to qualify for a green card. Recall that a green card is a much sought-after item that turns an undocumented immigrant into a legal resident alien who has the right to live and work in this country. Under U.S. immigration law, housework and child care are among the few jobs that permit employers to sponsor immigrants for green cards, making domestic service one of the only ways that women without relatives in the United States can legalize their status.

The law requires immigrant women to have had prior child care experience since most of those being sponsored for green cards take care of young children, while sponsoring families must demonstrate a moderately high income. In 2005 new regulations issued by the U.S. Department of Labor upgraded the category for live-in domestic workers from unskilled to skilled workers. The only catch is that the employer must prove that employing a live-in household worker is a business necessity.

The system is ripe for abuse. Once the papers are filed, it takes at least two or three years and $3,000 or more in legal fees before a green card is issued. During this time immigrant women are in legal limbo, bound to their current employers and without other job options. No matter what the conditions of employment, the promise of a green card is a powerful incentive to stay with the sponsoring family. In effect, then, immigration law helps mitigate the shortage of domestics in this country and dampens demands for state support of child care by providing a large pool of relatively cheap and docile workers to help meet the domestic needs of some high-income American families (Colen 1990).

Except for those being sponsored for green cards, live-in domestic work is typically a brief stage in the lives of Brazilian immigrant women in New York City. After a few months or a year they leave the homes of their employers and rent apartments, which they usually share with other immigrants. But most continue to work as housekeepers, baby sitters, or nannies, although now on a "live-out" basis. The ideal is to be employed five days a week by a few individuals or families, cleaning each apartment or house once or twice a week. For those willing to put in the hours, the work can pay quite well. In her research on Brazilian immigrants in Boston, Cristina Martes (2000) found that, of all immigrants, women doing housecleaning were earning the most consistent incomes and were best able to save money. She notes, for example, that a woman who cleans two houses a day at $50 a house, can take home $500 a week or $2,000 a month, a very comfortable sum by Brazilian standards. In fact, by 2007 in Framingham, Massachusetts, the site of a large Brazilian community, Brazilian owners of house-cleaning businesses—with the help of hired assistants—could make as much as $8,000 a month (Marcus 2008).

Still, domestic service shares many of the disadvantages of other low-wage service jobs. It is hard work, for one. Women often told me how, after eight or nine hours of cleaning kitchens and bathrooms, washing floors, dusting, vacuuming, and doing several loads of laundry, they arrived home too exhausted to do anything but take to their beds. Domestic work also offers little job security. When individuals or families go away on holiday or summer vacation, the "cleaning lady" is not needed, and Brazilians complain about the uncertainty and seasonality of the work. Many said their income falls dramatically during the summer months. Others told of a sudden drop in pay when one employer or another deemed their apartments in less frequent need of cleaning or worse, still, that they could not afford a housekeeper's services at all. Moreover, those employed in housework and private child care almost never receive fringe benefits and their wages are nearly always paid off the books.

Such are the penalties that come with working in the informal economy. Still, other than shoeshining, street vending, and some restaurant work, the only jobs employing large numbers of Brazilians that almost never require a green card are those in domestic service. To be sure, one has to know some English and have strong personal references, but these are easily supplied because domestic service jobs are passed back and forth between friends and relatives within the immigrant community. Despite the tirades against "illegal aliens," then, New Yorkers looking for someone to clean an apartment or to care for their children rarely ask about a prospective employee's legal status. And, as Brazilian immigrants are quick to point out, most Americans have absolutely no idea what a green card looks like anyway!

Serving New York

"Would you like some fresh ground pepper on your Caesar salad?" inquires the food handler[5] in an upscale Manhattan restaurant. The chances are excellent that the employee asking this question is an immigrant and, very possibly, an undocumented immigrant at that. This was brought home to me one evening when I noticed that the service was unusually slow at a trendy new restaurant in one of New York's public parks. It is a full-service restaurant and waiters scuttled about, but oddly no busboys were there to assist them, carry food trays, or clear away dirty dishes. When I asked our waiter about this he said that the restaurant indeed had tried to hire bus-boys but could not find anyone to take these jobs because "they pay so little," $2.00 an hour plus a percentage of the tips. The restaurant is owned by a large corporation that won a much publicized right to open in a public park by promising to charge moderate prices. Both its high profile and of-ficial connection to the city would make it unseemly, and probably risky, for the restaurant to hire undocumented immigrants for its low-wage posi-tions. Hence, the absence of busboys. After all, who but those with no other options would agree to work for such paltry wages?

This tale highlights the critical role immigrants play in the restaurant industry, the single most important source of employment in New York for *all* immigrants. And restaurant work is one of the fastest-growing job categories in the country. In the thirty-year period between 1964 and 1994 the number of restaurant workers went from 1.7 million to 7.1 million; by 2005 there were an estimated 12.5 million such workers (Johnston 1995; Ruiz 2005).

These figures are reflected in the employment profile of New York's Bra-zilian immigrant community, where restaurant work is to Brazilian men what domestic service is to Brazilian women. Nearly half of the men in my research sample worked in restaurants at one time or another since com-ing to New York, making restaurant work by far the largest source of male employment. Just as live-in domestic positions are common among Brazil-ian women when they are new to the city, one-third of the men in my study listed busboy or dishwasher as their first job.

Brazilians, like most recent immigrants, are hired for the unskilled and semi-skilled positions in full-service restaurants. But while busing tables and washing dishes are the most frequent restaurant jobs held by Brazilian immigrants, they are not the only ones. Food preparation and food service in upscale Manhattan restaurants involve many workers doing a variety of tasks. Aside from chefs and their assistants, there are kitchen cleaners, including dishwashers, salad makers who wash and prepare greens, waiters who recite the daily specials and take food and drink orders, food assem-blers who carry completed orders from the kitchen and assemble them on trays, food handlers who set dishes before customers and dispense bread, fresh pepper, and grated cheese, and busboys who fill water glasses and remove dirty dishes. There are also food buyers, restaurant managers, maitre'ds, bartenders, reservationists, coat checkers, and rest room atten-dants. The last two are the only restaurant jobs in which Brazilian women are usually employed.

A sprinkling of Brazilian immigrants are found in nearly all of these positions in New York restaurants and a few of them have managed to move up the job ladder. In fact, the restaurant industry is the city's only industry employing large numbers of Brazilians that provides immigrants with any real opportunity for upward mobility. Restaurant jobs lead upward from the bottom-ranked kitchen cleaner, through dishwasher, busboy, food assembler, food handler, to waiter. Waiting on tables is the top position held by most Brazilians employed in restaurants, although a few have made it to cook, bartender, food buyer, and maitre'd.

Some New York City restaurants have strong immigrant employment networks in which hiring is done almost exclusively through immigrant connections. Word of a job opening spreads rapidly among the restaurant's employees and a job seeker from the immigrant community is quickly found to take the position. New York's Brazilian immigrants dominate labor recruitment in several restaurants. One is a large midtown Manhattan restaurant featuring southwestern cuisine. On any given day about thirty Brazilians can be found working there as dishwashers, busboys, waiters, bartenders, cooks, hostesses, food buyers, and the like. The first Brazilian was hired in the mid-1980s and over the years, through word-of-mouth recruitment, somewhere between two and three hundred Brazilians have found jobs there.

Once such immigrant employment networks are set up, they often become self-perpetuating, even branching out to new establishments. For example, when the owner of the restaurant mentioned above opened a second restaurant, it too was quickly staffed by friends and relatives of current Brazilian employees. The downside of such networks is that they can effectively exclude members of other ethnic and racial groups or other immigrant communities from finding employment in the labor market niches they monopolize.

Driving New York

One image of New York that many visitors to the city retain long after they leave are the loudly honking, bright yellow taxicabs that cruise Manhattan streets in search of fares. Less well known, but equally important for transporting city residents, are the fleets of radio call cars that ply New York's outer boroughs, particularly Queens and Brooklyn, picking up passengers who have phoned radio dispatchers to request cars. This, too, is an immigrant-dominated industry and one in which many (male) Brazilians work.

After restaurant work, driving a radio call car was the second most common job among the Brazilian immigrant men in my study.

Legally, radio call car drivers can only transport passengers who have phoned in requesting pick-ups. As such, all drivers are affiliated with car service companies that employ dispatchers to answer the calls and direct drivers to the addresses of waiting customers. Most Brazilian drivers work for one of several car service companies owned by fellow Brazilians in Queens and these companies, in turn, employ mainly Brazilian drivers.

The life of a radio call car driver in New York City is not an easy one. In order to take home what they consider reasonable pay, Brazilian drivers must follow grueling twelve-hour-a-day, six-day-a-week schedules because their expenses are so high—fees to the car service company, insurance, gas, car repairs, and parking tickets. Moreover, driving a call car comes with an added worry not common to most jobs: crime. New York's tabloid press regularly carries stories about radio call car drivers—almost invariably male immigrants—being mugged or even murdered.

Despite these drawbacks many Brazilian men prefer driving radio call cars to other types of work. For one, it is a flexible job; a driver can make his own hours and be his own boss. It also pays quite well by Brazilian standards. A driver willing to put in many hours can regularly take home $600 a week. This work has another advantage. More than most jobs open to new immigrants, it conforms to middle-class Brazilian norms of what constitutes "suitable" work. To be sure, driving a cab is not something an educated person in Brazil would do, but unlike domestic service and restaurant employment, it lacks the taint of manual labor. As I noted earlier, in Brazil working with one's hands is a badge of lower-class status. This association is so strong that middle-class Brazilians find their American counterparts' penchant for hobbies like gardening or carpentry very peculiar indeed. Brazil's "gentleman's complex," the ideology that denigrates manual labor and those who engage in it, is one that Brazilians do not easily shed even as immigrants (Freyre 1964; Margolis, Bezerra, and Fox 2001).

Selling New York

The quintessential first job for Brazilians in New York City is street vending. Even more than live-in housekeeping and unskilled restaurant work, selling books, food, and other items on the city's sidewalks is tailor-made for newcomers. It requires very little English—not much more than giving the price of one's wares. It is largely unregulated and it requires no documents, not even a Social Security card. Street selling is a gender neutral job, the only one that employs roughly equal numbers of female and male immigrants. But it is also a job that most immigrants leave behind as soon as they find employment elsewhere. My research suggests that more than 90 percent of Brazilian street vendors had been in New York less than six months and that street selling for three or four months was typical before they moved on to other work.

Street vending is seen as undesirable for many reasons. For one, it requires work outdoors in all kinds of weather. Street vendors only pack up their wares and head home in heavy downpours, snowstorms, or when the thermometer edges down toward zero—Celsius. On clear, but frigid winter days they are seen stamping their feet in a vain effort to stay warm, and tales of frozen fingers and benumbed toes make the rounds in the immigrant community. For Brazilians used to their land's tropical and semi-tropical climes, such conditions are particularly onerous, but they have no choice but to put up with them because they receive no pay if they stay indoors. Then, there are the very long hours. Ten-hour days are typical for book sellers who begin at 8:00 or 9:00 a.m. and work until 6:00 or 7:00 p.m. Those selling food—hot dogs, soft pretzels, cold drinks, sugared nuts—have somewhat shorter hours since food sales only pick up at mid-day.

Street vendors' long hours spent at the mercy of the elements are not rewarded by hefty earnings. Since the income from street sales varies widely with the weather and the season, it is more irregular and more uncertain than the income from any other job that Brazilian immigrants hold. Vendors say that under icy wintry conditions pedestrians hurry by, not bothering to stop for a hotdog or a pretzel or to leaf through their displays of large "coffee table" books. Food sales pick up as temperatures moderate and are best on balmy spring and summer days. Book sales take off in November and December as the holidays approach.

Even in the best of times the income from these activities is not very attractive to Brazilian immigrants trying to earn as much money in as little time as possible. For book sellers, earnings usually range from $40 to $50 a day, although they can be quite a bit more during the frenzied pre-Christmas shopping season. Still, it is difficult to generalize about average income because it literally changes with the weather. For example, in a week of six sunny days, a food vendor can earn $350 to $400, but with three days of rain, income can be as little as $150 or $200. Thus, street vending has all the disadvantages of the low-wage, service jobs open to immigrants, especially those new to this country. Just imagine a job in which, day after day, you put in long hours standing on a street corner in all kinds of weather not knowing how much money you are going to earn for all your effort. It is little wonder, then, that at the first opportunity Brazilian immigrants give up their jobs on the streets for something a little better paying and more secure, usually indoors.

Building New York

An article on Brazilian immigrants in *Veja*, a Brazilian newsmagazine similar to *Time*, reported that immigrants from Governador Valadares were sometimes hired in teams by labor contractors in the United States. One man from the town, for example, headed a work crew of about fifteen of his fellow citizens who painted bridges in New Jersey. "This is a very closed market," he is quoted as saying. "The only way to get these positions is through labor contractors." Although now back home in Brazil, he still receives calls from American labor contractors seeking workers (Corrêa 1994:74).

Brazilian immigrants who work in construction in New York City are far less organized than their compatriots from Governador Valadares, that famed exporter of *brazucas* (Portuguese slang for Brazilians living in the United States), nor do they paint bridges. Brazilians in the city's construction industry do a variety of unskilled jobs involved in home and office painting and renovation. Some also work in demolition, paving, cement mixing, brick making, and hauling building materials. In New York City about as many Brazilian men work in construction as drive radio call cars, and in New York's suburbs, construction and renovation jobs, along with jobs in landscaping, are probably the single most important source of male employment. Brazilians are but one of many newcomers to New York who work in construction, where there is a strong immigrant presence in those parts of the building industry that are unlicensed and not unionized. In fact, on a national scale somewhere between 20 and 25 percent of the entire construction labor force in the United States, including jobs in renovation, painting, and other home improvements, is composed of undocumented immigrants (Freedman 1983; Farzad 2005).

Neither Brazilians nor other recent immigrants work in the skilled unionized building trades—as masons, electricians, carpenters, and so on.[6] Without connections, skilled union jobs are difficult to come by even for American citizens, and Brazilian immigrants in New York rarely have the training to be employed in them anyway. Recall that most Brazilian immigrants in the city had white-collar or professional jobs in Brazil and that from the Brazilian perspective, manual labor, even skilled manual labor, signifies humble status.

Most of the construction jobs available to undocumented immigrants are short-term, and layoffs and job changes are frequent. Another disadvantage of this work is the seasonality of many jobs in the industry. Construction in New York involving work outdoors usually drops off from about mid-December to mid-March and Brazilians scramble to find other temporary jobs. A few lucky Brazilians whose green cards permit them to come and go from the United States as they please simply head south to summer in Brazil, where the seasons are the reverse of those in the United States.

Brazilian Specialties

If you were asked about "typical jobs" for immigrants new to the United States, you might mention some of those already named—dish washing and busing tables, housekeeping and child care, perhaps driving a cab. But aside from this familiar terrain, Brazilian immigrants in New York City also dominate two other job niches that certainly would not come to mind: shoeshining and go-go dancing. While the number of Brazilian immigrants who shine shoes or dance in bars is relatively small, in Brazil's mass media and the nation's psyche, shoeshining and go-go dancing loom large as the archetypical work of their immigrant compatriots in the United States. That shoeshine "boys" and go-go "girls" represent immigrant employment in Brazilian discourse rests not on their numbers but on their dominance in these two small corners of the city's labor market. In the 1990s Brazilian men had a near monopoly—perhaps 90 percent—of the shoeshining jobs in the shoe repair shops and shoeshine stands that dot Manhattan, and Brazilian women reigned supreme as go-go dancers during those years, at one time holding up to 80 percent of such jobs in bars in New York City and throughout the metropolitan area.

As with most jobs that Brazilian immigrants hold, figures are illusive. What is certain is that shoe shining employs only a small fraction of Brazilians compared, for example, to restaurant work. While many Brazilian men work as shoeshiners, far more wash dishes and bus tables. It also stands to reason that the demand for go-go dancers is minuscule compared to the job market for live-in housekeepers, maids, and nannies, so that far fewer Brazilian women earn their living as dancers than as domestic servants.

How did Brazilians come to dominate these two small domains in the city's sprawling labor market? Once again, Governador Valadares takes center stage. The roots of Brazilian shoeshiners date all the way back to the mid-1960s when, through a migratory path that remains unclear, two brothers from that city found jobs as shoeshiners in midtown Manhattan. Word filtered back of the money to be made and by the end of the decade a tiny contingent of Brazilians were shining shoes in the vicinity of Grand Central Terminal. Their numbers slowly increased as networks of friends and relatives found shoeshine jobs for new arrivals in the city, and by the 1980s this job sector—once the domain of African Americans—was monopolized by Brazilians.

The route by which Brazilian immigrants came to dominate New York's go-go dancing jobs follows the same improbable path. Women from Governador Valadares began arriving in New York in the late 1960s or early 1970s, perhaps at the behest of male shoeshining relatives. At first the women were employed as domestic servants at modest salaries, but soon one or more found jobs dancing in bars—work that paid three times what they had been making as housecleaners. Word of these earnings made its way back to Brazil and other would-be dancers arrived. The flow of immigrant go-gos continued through the 1980s as women were lured by the prospect of earning $400 or $500 a week. Some dancers fanned out of the city and found work at bars in the New York suburbs and in New Jersey.

It is impossible to say how many Brazilian women are employed as go-go dancers in bars and nightclubs in the region. One Brazilian—a pioneer go-go dancer herself back in the 1970s—estimated that there are between two thousand and three thousand go-go dancers throughout the greater New York metropolitan area and that until the early 1990s, some 70 to 80 percent were Brazilian. Since then, Russian immigrant women have made major inroads into the profession.

But whatever the actual number, go-go dancing is still the most lucrative career track available to Brazilian immigrant women. In what other job can new immigrants, especially those without work papers, earn $300, $350, even $400 a night? The earnings of go-go dancers vary by bar, by the generosity of their clientele, and by the number of days and hours they are willing to work. Since income is from both wages and tips, it fluctuates widely although most dancers average about $200 a night.

Income from that other Brazilian forte, shining shoes, is not nearly as high as it is from go-go dancing, but it is still appealing to people used to Brazilian pay scales. Most of what shoeshiners earn comes from tips since the shoeshine stands and shoe repair shops that employ them either pay nothing at all or a nominal $10 to $15 a day. Because of this wage structure, income from this job, like that of so many others open to undocumented immigrants, swings wildly. It varies with the time of year and the weather—when it rains or snows, customers disappear. A shoeshiner's income ultimately depends on how many regular customers he has and how generous they are with their tips. On a busy day, a man with many steady customers working in a well-located shop can earn $80 or $90, although most average around $60 a day or $300 a week. In both go-go dancing and shoeshining, wages are paid in cash, as are tips, so that the income from them is "off-the-books." Thus, the figures cited refer to net income.

Aside from Brazilians who ply their trade at the city's shoe repair shops and shoeshine stands, some are employed as independent shoeshiners who cater to businessmen with offices in Manhattan skyscrapers. One enterprising Brazilian shoeshiner even set up a web site on which businessmen requiring his services can set up appointments (Menai 2007). Many immigrants prefer this work to shining shoes in stores or kiosks because the independent gets to keep not only his tips but the money the customer pays for the shoeshine as well. Moreover, working hours can be shorter and more flexible than those at a street-level shop, and independents also delight in the fact that they are their own bosses and can work the days and hours that they wish.

Both shoeshiners and go-go dancers work long hours for their pay. A shoeshiner's day starts at 7:00 to 7:30 a.m. and does not end until the last customer leaves with a shine on his shoes about 6:00 p.m. Go-go dancers usually come to work at 8:00 or 9:00 p.m. and stay until 3:00 or 4:00 a.m. Of course, the women are not dancing all of this time. A dancer will do a set of twenty or thirty minutes, usually accompanied by one or two other dancers. Then she will change clothes and may sit at the bar drinking or chatting with patrons while other dancers perform the next set. She then changes back into her costume and dances again. A shift lasts anywhere from five to eight hours, but go-go dancers intent on earning money quickly can work double shifts since some bars open around noon and have continuous performances until closing time in the wee hours of the morning.

All of this appears straightforward enough, but go-go dancing, more than any other job held by Brazilian immigrants, is a very problematic calling. Evidence for this comes from the fact that in conversations with me, Brazilian men were no more reluctant to discuss shining shoes than washing dishes or doing other menial jobs, while Brazilian women employed as go-go dancers were loath to talk about their work. The difficulty I had interviewing these women strongly suggests that most of them do not view go-go dancing as just another job. And if they feel constrained talking about their work with a nosy American researcher, they are even more evasive with their friends and relatives in Brazil, often telling them that the good money they earn comes from long hours spent "cleaning apartments" or "baby sitting."

Go-go dancers work in a predominantly male environment. Bar patrons usually are all men, and the only women in the bars are the dancers themselves and perhaps a barmaid. The bars in which dancers work vary by neighborhood. There are "sleazy" bars and "upscale" bars; the two are distinguished by their location, their clientele, and their general ambience. The jurisdiction in which a bar is located also affects working conditions. Striptease, for example, is legal in New York but not in New Jersey. In that state women may not dance topless—instead they wear tiny string bikinis. And bar owners cannot insist that dancers mingle with customers after the show. New York puts fewer legal restrictions on performers and topless dancing is standard. Dancers who work in go-go bars in Manhattan are generally expected to encourage patrons to buy drinks, and in some establishments they get a percentage of each drink sold.

Go-go dancers' extreme reluctance to discuss their employment is understandable given the seaminess of their work and its dark aura of degradation. Dancers are often subject to harassment. Most complain about being ongoing targets of sexual advances and lewd remarks. They are pawed by drunken patrons and constantly fend off unwanted proposals from customers who lie in wait for them outside the bars when they get off work. Both patrons and male bar employees hound them for dates, viewing go-go dancers as fair game by virtue of their occupation. These attitudes and actions reflect the stereotype that go-go dancers are nothing but prostitutes in disguise and that many abuse drugs as well. Most Brazilian dancers and their friends vigorously deny these allegations, insisting that few, if any, of their compatriots engage in such behavior. But whatever the case may be—and data on illicit activities are obviously difficult to come by—the image persists and it is the basis for go-go dancers' profound unease when questioned about their profession.

Going It Alone

"The Brazilian community is mostly one of employees, not employers," I was told soon after I began my field research in New York City. And, for the most part, this turned out to be true. Brazilian immigrants have no entrepreneurial niche like that of the Korean greengrocer, the Indian newsstand dealer, or the Mexican flower seller. Most Brazilian immigrants, at least at first, see themselves as sojourners, not permanent settlers in the city, making them more likely to "take the money and run," as one Brazilian put it, than to invest in a future in the United States.

Although they are the exception, not the rule, there are Brazilian immigrants who have started businesses in New York, some of which have become very successful. Little Brazil, the block-long street in midtown Manhattan, the commercial heart of the Brazilian community, has several immigrant entrepreneurs—owners of restaurants and remittance and travel agencies—albeit ones who arrived in the city some four decades ago. More modest Brazilian-owned businesses that cater almost exclusively to the immigrant community are located in Astoria, Queens, the city's primary Brazilian residential neighborhood. Here newsstands, grocery stores, and small shops carry all manner of items from back home—Brazilian newspapers and magazines, CDs and videos, Brazilian brands of beer and soft drinks, *farinha de mandioca* (manioc flour), a staple of the Brazilian diet, even tiny Brazilian-made string bikinis called "dental floss" (*fio dental* in Portuguese). A variety of restaurants and snack bars offer Brazilian specialties like *pão de queijo* (cheese buns) and *frango a passarinho* (garlicky Brazilian fried chicken). There are also beauty salons with a largely Brazilian clientele, travel agencies featuring flights to Rio de Janeiro and São Paulo, and remittance agencies that guarantee next-day delivery of immigrants' hard-earned dollars to waiting relatives back in Brazil.

Astoria is also home base to several Brazilian-owned radio call car companies, one of the city's few enterprises started by Brazilian immigrants that do not have an exclusively Brazilian clientele. The companies' immigrant founders themselves worked as call car drivers and then set up dispatcher services used by other drivers. Stretch limousines—upscale variants of radio call cars—are also available for hire from two thriving enterprises, both founded by Brazilian immigrants.

Then there are the Brazilians who have shunned pedestrian enterprises aimed at their fellow ethnics, preferring instead to hitch their entrepreneurial stars to the growing popularity of things Brazilian. *Capoeira*, the popular Brazilian martial art, is taught by Brazilians in a number of upscale sports clubs in the city. In recent years New York also has been awash with Brazilian performers and musicians. Well-known Brazilian talents often perform at Lincoln Center, Carnegie Hall, or some less famous venue.

Free concerts of Brazilian music in Central Park draw not only Brazilian natives, but scores of American aficionados as well. More than a dozen restaurants and nightclubs in Manhattan have responded to this vogue by featuring Brazilian food and music. Particularly popular are *churrascarias*, Brazilian-style barbecue restaurants. Two or three expatriate bands travel the metropolitan New York nightclub circuit playing Brazilian *samba*, *bossa nova*, and *forró*, and companies of Brazilian singers, dancers, and musicians have been formed to capitalize on the Brazilian music craze. A nearly all-Brazilian cast of twenty-five dancers and musicians sporting elaborate Carmen Miranda–like costumes performs several shows a month at private parties, bar mitzvahs, nightclubs, and carnival balls around the New York metropolitan area.

While acknowledging the entrepreneurs of Little Brazil and Astoria, many of the city's long-time Brazilian residents lament the general lack of business acumen among their newly arrived compatriots. "Why is it that Koreans, Indians, and Chinese all have booming businesses, while Brazilians have nothing?" they ask with evident chagrin, apparently unaware of several other business ventures, both large and small, started by fellow Brazilians. There is, for example, the couple that sells Brazilian items at the city's street fairs and the dozen or so Brazilian women who do catering from their apartments in Queens. These and other mundane Brazilian-owned enterprises—a delivery service, an auto body shop, an electronics repair shop, a paving company, a towing service, a painting company—escape the notice of most Brazilian residents. Since these small businesses encompass a multiplicity of money-making ventures, they are easily overlooked.

There are also a handful of Brazilian immigrants who have "made it big" in businesses in the city that have nothing to do with their ethnic roots. There is the owner of an upscale Manhattan furniture store, for example, and the proprietor of a chic beauty salon. There is the clothes designer with her own shop in Soho and the manufacturer of pricey handbags sold in New York department stores. Then there is the society florist, the interior designer, and the art gallery owner—Brazilian immigrants all turned entrepreneurs.

This, then, is a sketch of the low-wage service sector in which most Brazilians and so many other new immigrants find themselves. We can now understand why the labor of new immigrants, whether documented or not, is sought after by employers in this segment of the American economy. Immigrants are valued not only because of the relatively low cost of their labor, but because of the temporary nature of their migration. At least at first, most immigrants view their stay in the United States as short term. And so, however much they may deny it, Brazilians and other international migrants are sought by American employers. As an abundant source of inexpensive but often well-educated labor, they are an employer's dream: workers who are willing, even eager, to take a variety of jobs that otherwise might go unfilled.

But taking menial jobs carries a price. Brazilian immigrants in New York do work that would be considered "way beneath them" back home. How do they deal with this social descent? And how do they adjust to being new immigrants in the maelstrom of one of the world's greatest cities? These are the subjects of the next chapter.

Long lines form early as Brazilians seeking tourist visas to the United States wait outside the U.S. consulate in Rio de Janeiro. All photographs courtesy of Jerald Milanich.

Money earned by Brazilians in the United States funds construction booms like this one in Governador Valadares, an "emigrant-sending community."

Little Brazil Street (West 46th Street) in New York City caters to both Brazilian immigrants and Brazilian tourists.

A Brazilian-owned restaurant in Astoria, Queens, the primary residential neighborhood of Brazilian immigrants in New York City.

Shelves in stores in Brazilian residential neighborhoods are lined with products imported from home.

The lively Brazilian Street Fair on New York's Little Brazil Street in late summer draws Brazilians from all over the northeastern United States.

T-shirts celebrating Brazilian ethnicity and *saudades* (longing for home) are sold at the Brazilian Street Fair.

Brazilians in elaborate Carnival costumes participate in parades and street fairs in New York City.

Immigrant Life in Gotham City

The life of Brazilians, like that of so many other immigrants new to New York City, is fraught with challenges and hardship. Brazilian immigrants not only have to come to terms with working at low-status, menial jobs that would be unthinkable back home, but they also have to weather the long hours of drudgery that the jobs often entail. They have to contend with a dizzying cacophony of English—a language few newcomers speak with any fluency—as they move around an alien metropolis with its baffling transportation hubs, frenzied street life, and daunting pace. They have to deal with the high cost of living in a city that bills itself "the capital of the world" as they find a place to live and forge a modest existence, all the while trying to save as much money as possible for the return home.

As if all this were not enough, many immigrants also worry about their undocumented status, constantly looking over their shoulders for the fearsome specter of "Tia Mimi" (Aunt Mimi), Portuguese slang for the U.S. Immigration and Naturalization Service.[1] And perhaps hardest of all, these experiences are lived under the poignant shadow of *saudades*, "the memories which touch a soul," the aching longing for home, for family and friends, for the familiar (Feldman-Bianco 1992:45).

The Fall from Grace

One of the first harsh facts of New York life that recent arrivals from Brazil have to face is the profound loss of status that accompanies their employment. Given their largely middle-class roots and the negative eye with which Brazilians from this social stratum view manual labor, it is little wonder that they suffer from their downward social track, finding it one of their most difficult crosses to bear as immigrants.

Take domestic service as an example. In Brazil, class differences are often displayed in manner and attitude. Domestic servants, who are near the bottom of the nation's social scale, are expected to be submissive in exchanges with their employers. This dance of deference requires that servants stand passively in their employer's presence and generally not speak until spoken to. They address their *patrões* (bosses) with heads slightly bowed and eyes lowered, always using the respectful terms *o senhor* and *a senhora*—the formal male and female forms of "you" in Portuguese—when talking to them. Servants, in turn, are called *você* by their employers, the more familiar form of "you" used in addressing children and between close friends and relatives.

Just imagine what such work means to a middle-class Brazilian in New York who suddenly finds herself transformed into a domestic servant. Back home it is she who would be the employer since nearly all middle-class families in Brazil have household help. Time and again during the course of my research I encountered just such women—lawyers, social workers, engineers, psychologists, and teachers—working as live-in housekeepers, day maids, and baby sitters. The disdainful treatment of domestic workers in Brazil, the menial nature of their jobs, and the profound inequality inherent in the employer-servant dyad all contribute to making domestic service highly problematic for Brazilian immigrants. For the middle-class Brazilian woman working as a domestic, the breach between her social roots and her current occupation makes for a crash course in downward mobility.

Brazilian women cope with their degraded status in various ways. Some use humor. Women joke about how incompetent they are at housework; after all, they had servants to do it in Brazil. Others try to compartmentalize their life and work by putting themselves in a sort of disassociative state when they are scrubbing floors or doing laundry. Still others take great pains to conceal the nature of their jobs from family members in Brazil. But the conviction that such work is short-term is what gets most of them through the day. Because a majority of Brazilians, at least initially, come to the United States as sojourners, not as settlers, they are more easily reconciled to their menial jobs and the accompanying loss of status that they bring. They view both the jobs and their social descent as temporary.

There is, however, one arrangement that belies the general pattern of downward mobility associated with domestic service. The researcher Cristina Martes (2000) found that some Brazilian immigrants in Boston are in the business of selling their house-cleaning jobs. This is how it works: A Brazilian cleans a number of houses on a regular basis and decides to return to Brazil. She spreads the word in the Brazilian community that she is "selling" the houses where she works. When a buyer appears, the job seller tells her employer that she is returning to Brazil and that a friend or relative—a person of great trust—is interested in taking over the job. For a month or so the two go to the employer's house together, during which time the job seller explains the work routine to the buyer, who also meets the prospective employer, who is completely unaware that the job is being "sold." If the would-be buyer is acceptable to the employer the transaction is completed. The typical price per house is the money earned cleaning it over a three-month period, a sum that can amount to $1,500 to $3,000 or more depending on how frequently it is cleaned.

In another arrangement housecleaners with several houses to clean sub-contract assistants—usually more recently arrived Brazilians—and in so doing become employers in their own right and, in effect, business owners. Depending on the number of homes cleaned, such cleaning entrepreneurs with many assistants can earn considerable sums of money (Millman 2006). As such, a case can be made that for some immigrants, housecleaning—despite its low status in Brazil—can be transformed into a way up the social and economic ladder in the United States.

Domestic service is not the only occupation held by Brazilian immigrants that usually means a sharp decline in rank. Restaurant employment also impairs social standing and causes similar anxiety among male immigrants. In Brazil work as a waiter or busboy would be out of the question for anyone with much more than a primary school education, but in New York I met Brazilians with professional degrees busing tables and washing dishes. And, despite what can be excellent pay in upscale Manhattan restaurants, in Brazil such jobs have the dual taints of low wages and low status, and most Brazilian immigrants continue to see them in the same light, albeit in a new setting.

For some immigrants, particularly those here for the long-term, mobility may not be a one-way street. That is, immigration can mean a move up the social ladder. There is, for example, the immigrant who began transporting goods with a small rented van. In time his business grew and today he has more than ten trucks making deliveries around the New York metropolitan area (Menai 2007). There is also the Brazilian couple with two American-born children who worked their way up from sous-chef and housecleaner to owners of a highly rated Brazilian restaurant in Queens. Then there is the divorced woman who had managed an upscale clothing store in São Paulo. She was also a licensed cosmetologist but never practiced her craft in Brazil. After arriving in New York in 1999 she worked as a housekeeper, babysitter, and cleaned a beauty salon. Today, now documented and happily married to an American, she owns her own small hair salon in midtown Manhattan.

Strangers in a Strange Land

Aside from what they must endure at work, Brazilian immigrants—like all new immigrants—are subject to a daily barrage of shocks to their sense of the familiar. The lack of proficiency in English does not make things any easier. Sixty percent of the Brazilians in my study rated their English as "fair to poor," while only 13 percent said it was "excellent or fluent." Just imagine being in their position, living amid the meaningless swirl of an unknown language in a foreign culture. "People who don't speak English suffer a lot in New York," one Brazilian told me. "To come here without speaking English is suicide," another said. Some blamed the solitude that many immigrants feel in the United States on their lack of fluency in English; without it they cannot fully participate in the bustling life that surrounds them.

The inability to speak English well and the sense of isolation and loneliness that that entails enhance feelings of alienation, especially among immigrants without relatives in New York. To live apart from one's family is always viewed as a hardship by Brazilians regardless of the reasons for the separation. When I was a graduate student and spent six weeks in Brazil doing research on a sugar estate in Bahia, Brazilians continually asked me how I could "bear to be so far away from my family for so long."

In this respect the contrast between life in Brazil and life in the United States is particularly striking. Aside from their immediate families, people in Brazil typically see other relatives—aunts, uncles, cousins, grandparents, in-laws, married siblings—on a regular, even a daily basis. Relatives tend to live near each other, and in large cities family members often have apartments in the same building (Miller 1979). Moreover, in Brazil—which lacks a tradition of "going away to college" or "going out on one's own"—adult children typically do not leave home until they marry. That many Americans go off to college in their late teens and early twenties or leave their parents to live alone or move in with friends is viewed as both odd and lamentable by Brazilian immigrants. *Why*, they ask, would anyone *want* to live apart from his or her family?

Recall that another American trait that Brazilians find strange is the desire for privacy. Social life in Brazil usually revolves around family members who think nothing of dropping in on each other unannounced. But, as Brazilian immigrants soon learn, one does not do that in the United States. The doors of people's houses are not open to friends and relatives like they are in Brazil. As one immigrant advises her newly arrived compatriots, "Americans value their privacy and you should never just show up at an American's home without making a date first."

Some culture shocks to an immigrant's sense of the familiar are more abstract. A common Brazilian plaint about New York involves its quality of life—its frenetic pace, the incivility of its salespeople and bus drivers, the anonymous crowds of subway riders, and the throngs of pedestrians jostling for space on cramped Manhattan sidewalks. Brazilians cite the avoidance of eye contact between strangers on the street, on the subway, or on the bus as odd or foreign or simply "un-Brazilian." This lack of engagement, in turn, is linked to a more encompassing complaint about the United States. The "American personality" is "cold," I was told, or at least "more restrained" compared to the "Brazilian personality." It lacks *calor humano*, an indefinable blend of human warmth and empathy (Margolis 2001).

Related to this lack of "human warmth" is the Brazilian complaint that Americans simply do not know how to enjoy themselves. On weekends and holidays "people go shopping instead of getting together with family and friends," I was told. "All the stores are open and the health clubs are full." Americans are either working or shopping, they say, not having fun.

But Brazilians also have high praise for certain aspects of American life and institutions, particularly in comparison with their counterparts back home. Brazilian immigrants in Boston, for example, put a positive spin on the respectful and "egalitarian" treatment they receive from merchants and local authorities in that city and this, they note, is despite their poor English and the questionable legal status of some. Many immigrants are impressed by what they perceive as the efficiency of social welfare and law enforcement in the United States. They also feel much less threatened by violence than they do in Brazil and have more confidence in the local police.[2] Then, too, they are favorably impressed by the relatively relaxed, easy-going relationship between employers and employees in the United States; it is "respectful" and "more professional" than in Brazil, they say, especially in the status minefield of domestic service. These sorts of positive, even idealized views of the host country are common among immigrants, particularly new arrivals (Martes 1996; Suárez-Orozco and Suárez-Orozco 1995).

Other immigrants value the laissez-faire, "do your own thing" attitude of New Yorkers. "You can wear what you like here and no one bothers you or criticizes you or even *looks* at you," a woman from Rio de Janeiro told me. And poor dress does not mean poor treatment, as it so often does in Brazil, where a man in work clothes or a woman in a housedress and flip flops will be left cooling their heels for hours in a doctor's waiting room or at a bank or government office, while a man in a suit and tie or an elegantly dressed woman will be immediately ushered in (Margolis 2001).

Of course, the opportunity to earn what Brazilian immigrants consider "good money" is often cited as a principal feature of American life. They also admire the apparent health of the U.S. economy, which, unlike the one they were once used to back home, has not been wracked by rampant inflation. To immigrants a stable economy means the ability to save and plan for the future, a near impossibility during Brazil's long inflation nightmare that finally ended in the mid-1990s. Then, too, some Brazilians are very taken with American buying power. To Brazilians the fact that an "ordinary" middle-class citizen—that is, one who is not rich—can simply go out and buy a color television set or a computer, without paying for it on time with hefty interest charges or planning for it months in advance, is enticing indeed.

There are also the singular attractions of living in "the capital of the world" with its kaleidoscope of peoples and cultures, pulsing street life, glittering skyline, and "canyons of steel." Brazilian immigrants also recounted the subtle appeals of urban life: the enchantment of a first snowfall, the experience of autumn in Central Park, a long-dreamed-of visit to the top of the Empire State Building, an evening bus ride down the dazzling neon wall of Broadway to Times Square. Some Brazilians were so taken with the delights of New York City that they sounded more like tourists on holiday than immigrants struggling to earn money in menial jobs. One immigrant, a widow from Rio de Janeiro, declared that she had "returned to life in New York." And another Brazilian pointed out that, while many of her compatriots go back to Brazil with the intention of staying, some turn right around and fly back to the United States because "New York is like a vice, people get addicted. They just keep coming back for more."

In Pursuit of *Verdinhas*

Brazilian immigrants in New York call U.S. dollars *verdinhas*, "little green things." Many say that earning and saving them are among the most difficult problems they face as immigrants because life in this country is so costly. The Brazilian media's images of the United States notwithstanding, immigrants soon learn that *verdinhas* do not grow on trees. Brazilians fault themselves and their compatriots for the mirage of the "easy buck," for their grand delusions about what a dollar buys and what it takes to earn. One immigrant likened Brazilians who come to New York to the poverty-stricken migrants of Brazil's Northeast who travel south to São Paulo on *pão de araras* ("parrot's perches," crowded open-air trucks) in search of jobs and a better life. Both migrant streams involve similar "deceptive dreams of riches," he said.

Brazilian immigrants often spoke of how they were deluded about the material realities of life in the United States. They talked of how foolish they were to believe that after working for two or three years in this country they could return home with $40,000 or $50,000 in savings. They recounted their naive faith in the absurd notion that someone could actually live on a minimum wage of $7.00 an hour in New York City, a figure that initially sounds like a lot of money to people from a country like Brazil where in 2008 the minimum wage was $250 *a month*. Many immigrants were also taken aback by the high cost of housing in the city and decried the steep rents they had to pay for even spartan dwellings.

In truth, there are probably fewer misconceptions about the earning power of new immigrants in the United States than the discourse of some Brazilians would suggest. I met very few immigrants who actually expected to return to Brazil, their pockets bulging with *verdinhas*. Most were more realistic about their likely savings; $10,000 or $20,000 over two to three years were the most common figures I heard. Moreover, immigrants' plans for the money were equally modest: to make a down payment on a piece of property in Brazil—a house, a condominium, some land, or a small business. For a few the goal was more immediate: to earn enough to send remittances to their families back home. However, it is indeed true that most immigrants were genuinely stunned by the high cost of living in New York City and we already know their responses to this reality: sharing living quarters and utilities, renting rooms to compatriots, spending the bare minimum on furnishings and clothing, and generally living as frugally as possible—at least during their first months in the city.

Brazilian immigrants in New York also undergo a quick reality check when they discover just how hard they have to work to achieve their goals. Given their relatively low wages, the expense of living in a world capital like New York, and their intention of saving money for the return home, Brazilians have to labor very long hours, indeed, often working at two jobs. Once again, words like "illusion" are used in reference to what making "good money" entails in a city like New York. Brazilians have "no real understanding of what it is like to work in the U.S.," I was told, because former migrants returning to Brazil "brag about how much money they earned. They make it sound so easy." As a result, the real-life experience of twelve- or thirteen-hour days comes as a shock, said one immigrant, contrasting this with the eight-hour day typical of middle-class jobs in Brazil. "So of course they suffer," he concluded.

On the Lookout

Were they aware of it, one piece of information that might brighten the lives of undocumented Brazilians and other "out of status" (undocumented) immigrants in New York City is that the U.S. Department of Homeland Security does little to track down visa overstayers. As we've seen, the only program, U.S.-Visit, to locate and presumably deport the estimated 150,000 "visitors" who overstay their tourist and student visas to the United States each year was only started in 2004. While this was meant to track visitors' entries and exits, three years after its implementation it still did little to track visitors leaving the country (Stana 2007). In fact, the department has devoted relatively few resources to this sector of the undocumented population.

Then, too, factories and sweatshops that employ undocumented Mexicans, Central Americans, and Chinese tend to be raided by the authorities rather than businesses—like restaurants—that employ immigrants from other nations (Irish, Poles, Brazilians, Canadians) who are undocumented because they overstay their visas. Finally, undocumented immigrants in New York City have even less to fear than those in some other parts of the country because since 1996 a city executive order has been in force that bans city agencies from notifying federal authorities about undocumented immigrants, if such notification would prevent them from enrolling their children in school, reporting a crime, or seeking medical aid (Hunt 1996; Schmitt 1996).

But these facts are unknown to most undocumented immigrants, including Brazilians, so the fear of apprehension and deportation is very real. Another reason undocumented Brazilians are fearful is because in Brazil everyone is required to carry a national identity card that must be presented to the authorities upon request. Most Brazilians are unaware that there is no equivalent document in the United States and that the New York police will not arbitrarily stop them on the street and demand to see their papers.

However, it is also true that occasional raids on sweatshops or other businesses employing large numbers of undocumented workers, including

Brazilians, do take place. For example, a raid on an office-cleaning business in Newark rounded up sixty undocumented workers from Brazil and Portugal (*Brazilian Voice* 1995). After September 11, 2001, there were also reports of stepped up immigration raids in some Massachusetts communities with large Brazilian populations (Abraham 2005a). Then there is the case of the shoeshine shop near Grand Central Station. Two years after completing my original research, I returned to the shop—long an employer of undocumented Brazilians—that I had visited many times before. Unprompted, the owner told me that he "had had to fire at least forty shoeshiners" when he "suddenly" found out he was employing "illegal aliens" who lacked green cards. He claimed that federal authorities had begun enforcing the law and that he is "in court" as a result. He now demands to see a green card or a Social Security card or he will not hire the person because "it's just not worth it." But, then he offered a caveat: "Since Americans won't do this work," he told me, he will still hire someone without papers, "if the shop is very busy."

Particularly after the attacks of September 11, the nation's burgeoning anti-immigrant discourse, so rife on U.S. airwaves, has also heightened distrust among those without papers. My own experience is illustrative. I noted a marked change in tone when I revisited several upscale Manhattan restaurants in which I had previously interviewed Brazilian employees. Where I had once been greeted with friendly curiosity as a Portuguese-speaking foreigner along with an apparent eagerness to engage in conversation, Brazilian employees now were very reluctant to talk to me. Although I again spoke Portuguese and only asked innocuous questions such as "Where do you come from in Brazil?" many appeared suspicious of my interest in them and cut short our conversation. Surely this change in behavior must have had something to do with the heated polemics that now envelop the hot button issue of "illegal aliens."

Even before the recent attention to undocumented immigration, however, fear of Tia Mimi affected the lives of many Brazilian immigrants in New York City. Anxiety about Tia Mimi is present almost from the moment that many would-be immigrants step off the plane at Kennedy Airport and pass through immigration inspection, where their motives for visiting this country may be questioned.

This anxiety continues to shadow Brazilian immigrants as they go about their lives in the city. Under the misconception that to do so would put them at risk, some undocumented Brazilians are reluctant to provide their local addresses when filling out forms of any kind—applications to open a bank account or to apply for a job or forms to send remittances to Brazil. For the same reason, some Brazilians avoid contact with the Brazilian consulate in New York City, erroneously assuming that consular personnel are obligated to turn undocumented immigrants over to the American authorities. Then, too, afraid to call attention to themselves, many are hesitant to report crimes against them to the New York police. Even living arrangements are colored by fear. One Brazilian suggested to me that his compatriots reside together in crowded apartments not just to save money but for security; they feel there is safety in numbers.

The apprehension surrounding their undocumented status, along with the burning desire to visit relatives and friends in Brazil—something immigrants without papers have found it increasingly difficult to do because they run a very high risk of not being allowed back into the United States—leads some Brazilians to spend thousands of dollars in the often fruitless quest for a green card. Unscrupulous lawyers are more than willing to take advantage of these fears. Self-styled "immigration counselors" prey on undocumented Brazilians and other immigrants and for fees of $3,000 and more "guarantee" to get them green cards through nonexistent "amnesty programs."

A somewhat more certain path to legalization is through marriage to an American citizen. While many such marriages are based on love and companionship, a significant but unknown number involve the pursuit of something else again: a green card. These so-called green card marriages, in which an immigrant marries for the sole purpose of obtaining a green card, most commonly involve a Brazilian marrying an American citizen of Hispanic origin, often a Puerto Rican. These arrangements are both costly and time consuming. The would-be American spouse receives $10,000 or more and the process takes at least three years. During this time the couple must submit to a series of interviews with immigration officers and demonstrate that they have filed joint tax returns. Then, when the immigrant has the green card in hand, and pays an additional hefty sum to an attorney, divorce papers are filed and the marriage is dissolved.

Parenthetically, in New York City about 1,200 people a month petition federal authorities for legal residency based on their marriage to American citizens. One immigration agent compared the separate interviews of spouses to the old TV show *Newlywed Game* because couples are questioned about the intimate details of their lives to determine if they actually live together. In the end, about 16 percent of those interviewed are denied green cards because federal agents believe the marriages to be fraudulent (Sontag 1994).

Ties That Do Not Bind

The uneasy suspicion of some in New York's Brazilian immigrant community that immigration agents lurk around every corner is tied to the premise that there are informers in their midst. I was told that the threat of "don't do that to me or I'll call Tia Mimi" was not an idle one and that more than a few Brazilians turned in their compatriots for monetary gain. Federal authorities purportedly pay $500 for useful tips on the whereabouts of undocumented workers. Still, I was unable to document a single case of Brazilians informing on one another to the authorities and I believe that, in fact, this rarely or never occurs.

Why, then, the prevailing notion that Brazilians betray each other? This is but one ingredient in the wide-ranging discourse among Brazilian immigrants about rampant "bad" behavior among their fellow ethnics in New York City. From my first day of field work, Brazilians bombarded me with an array of complaints about their compatriots. Again and again, I was told Brazilians "only think of themselves," "don't help each other," "cheat on each other," and "don't want other Brazilians to get ahead." Some immigrants declared that they had few or no Brazilian friends and that when they heard people speaking Portuguese they crossed the street to avoid them because they "don't want anything to do with Brazilians."

One recurrent theme in this discourse is that, in New York, Brazilians are transformed into their evil twins. They go from being generous, caring individuals to selfish, self-centered louts. "It's unfortunate that people become so cold and egotistical here," a Brazilian immigrant told me. Immigrants themselves blame neither the New York environment nor American institutions for this transformation. Rather, it is their own pursuit of the almighty dollar that is held responsible. "Immigrants begin to think only about money when they come here," another Brazilian said. "They live by a different ethic in the U.S. than they do in Brazil." Moreover, these complaints are not limited to Brazilian immigrants in New York City. In Miami, another major center of Brazilian immigration, one new arrival is quoted as saying, "It's not like it was in Brazil. Here everyone is for himself" (Neto and Bernardes 1996:56).

Examples of "bad" behavior were legion. I was told tales of Brazilians charging each other for carrying money back to their families in Brazil or for doing each other even the most minor favors. One immigrant recounted with disgust how another Brazilian—whom she had considered a friend—charged her a week's wages for finding her a job as a live-in housekeeper. Even though she detested the job and left after a week or two, her "friend" refused to return the finder's fee. Other stories of misbehavior involved "job stealing." According to one immigrant, when Brazilians see new compatriots arrive in New York, their first thought is, "Have they come to grab my job?"

While these allegations of boorish behavior are probably exaggerated, some softening of ethical standards does, in fact, occur. This is not due to any special failing of Brazilians as a national cohort, but rather to the immigrant experience itself. Research suggests that Brazilians are not the only immigrants decrying the change in their compatriots' behavior after they arrive in the United States. Immigrants from El Salvador living on New York's Long Island, for example, were dismayed that "the common courtesies and reciprocities of their home country lives had not migrated to the United States with them." While Salvadorans had expected to be exploited by Americans, "they did not come prepared to be taken advantage of by their own co-ethnic peers" (Mahler 1995:32, 102). And in a community of Russian Jewish immigrants in California, "feelings of distrust and individualism are pervasive," causing many émigrés to distance themselves from their compatriots (Gold 1995:90). The political scientist Michael J. Piore's stark portrait of the material motives that fuel the lives of most new immigrants helps explain these bitter complaints. Immigrants, he writes, "are people divorced from a social setting, operating outside the constraints and inhibitions that it imposes, working totally and exclusively for money" (Piore 1979:55). Obviously such single-minded determination is detrimental both to interpersonal relations and to community building.

Indeed, the Brazilian critique was not limited to individuals; it extended to Brazilians collectively and to local Brazilian institutions as well. "Brazilians are the most disunited ethnic group in the city," I was told. This declaration was repeated again and again by Brazilians who lamented the fact that, unlike many other immigrant groups in New York, Brazilians failed to cooperate with each other and to organize on their own behalf. A feeble community esprit de corps was blamed for the lack of Brazilian social clubs, community groups, and mutual aid societies.[3]

Once again, while Brazilians decry the absence of community organizations, they are by no means the only new immigrants who lack such institutions. For example, the author of a study of Israeli immigrants in New York notes that they "have not initiated even one viable institution of their own . . . not even one active voluntary association" (Shokeid 1988:53).

The issue of community among Brazilian immigrants and community-based institutions or rather, the lack thereof, has been dubbed "braspho-bia." In 2003 an informal conference with that title was organized by the Brazilian Rainbow Group in New York City. I gave a presentation there that analyzed what I call the "discourse of Brazilians bad mouthing each other" (Margolis 2003). Part of the discourse is the refusal of some Brazilians living in the United States to identify themselves as Brazilian. I found this in the Brazilian community in New York City and it also has been reported by researchers in Boston and Miami (Martes 2000; Resende 2002, 2005). As one immigrant in south Florida told the anthropologist Rosana Resende, who was inquiring about his nationality, "I *was* Brazilian."

One researcher has come up with an intriguing thesis concerning community and ethnic cohesion among Brazilian immigrants, arguing that Brazilians are less fragmented than they are "ethnically ambivalent" (Brown 2005a; 2005b). Such ambivalence refers to the celebration of "Brazilian-ness" among individuals and small groups of Brazilians with a simultaneous feeling of "alienation" toward this same "Brazilianness" when it comes to the Brazilian immigrant population at large. In other words, they express positive views of Brazilians individually and negative views of Brazilians collectively.

Brazilians have high regard for themselves and their compatriots, whom they believe possess a strong work ethic and general decency, but have negative views of Brazilians as employers and community leaders. This explains why, for example, Brazilians say they prefer American employers to Brazilian ones and are usually reluctant to participate in events organized by the larger community. Brazilian immigrants are not categorically disunited; rather they are conflicted and ambivalent. This results in the following paradox: Brazilians are very critical of other Brazilians, but at the same time their social networks consist almost exclusively of Brazilians.

Why this ethnic ambivalence? The key is the distinctively Brazilian notion of *jeitinho*, the uniquely Brazilian way of getting things done (Brown 2005b). It is a means of cutting through obstacles—such as rules and red tape—to achieve a desired end. In Brazil *jeitinhos* are partly a response to that nation's notorious bureaucratic thicket, which makes getting a government document, be it a driver's license, passport, or marriage certificate, a cumbersome process.

Within the immigrant context a *jeitinho* can be invaluable. It can "prove" that a would-be immigrant has the financial resources to secure a tourist visa by temporarily borrowing money from friends and relatives or, once in this country, it can help a Brazilian get a job even if he or she lacks work papers. But at times *jeitinhos* have the opposite effect and involve Brazilians taking advantage of one another—charging for advice about where to find employment, for example, or exploiting the ignorance of newly arrived compatriots about life in the big city. So *jeitinhos* can help Brazilians survive or they can create problems for them. As such, *jeitinhos* are both a "social glue and social repellent for Brazilians" (Brown 2005b:71). This is why the Brazilian community is not so much a fragmented one as a conflicted one, a community characterized by extremely polarized relationships—warm, loving, social ones among family and friends and highly suspicious, distant ones when it comes to unknown Brazilians and the Brazilian community writ large.

Brazilian immigrants themselves offered much simpler explanations for this dearth of unity and collective vitality. One woman, a longtime New York resident, blamed the city's burgeoning Brazilian population. When she first arrived in the city far fewer Brazilians were living there and since "everyone knew everyone else" this meant a greater sense of community solidarity. Another Brazilian cited the distrust that pervades any group with a large contingent of undocumented individuals. Fear of informers prevents an easygoing sociality with compatriots who are not close friends and relatives. Still other immigrants cited personalistic factors: the absence of dynamic, high-minded community leaders to unify Brazilians and promote their common interests.

Several Brazilians noted that in New York they not only lack a social community but a physical community as well, a distinctly Brazilian neighborhood to call their own. Even the block dubbed "Little Brazil" in Manhattan is theirs in name only.[4] Perhaps tied to the lack of a physical community is the underwhelming scale of Brazilian enterprises in New York City, that is, businesses that could provide newly arrived immigrants with jobs. Brazilians have no equivalent of the Korean green grocery or the Indian newsstand, no distinct occupational niche with which they are identified. And with no ready source of employment within their own community, there is no economic basis for ethnic solidarity (Bonacich and Modell 1980). It is quite the contrary, said one immigrant. The few Brazilians who do own businesses "not only are no help to new immigrants, they exploit them, pay them less and make them work longer hours."

Brazilian tradition also helps explain the paucity of social cohesion and local ethnic structures in New York. Brazil has a less-developed tradition of membership in clubs and mutual interest associations than does the United States. Notes the anthropologist Conrad P. Kottak, "The typical American belongs to dozens of non-kin based groups. These include churches, political parties, clubs, teams, occupational groups, [and] organizations. . . . In Brazil, where home and extended family hold their own so vigorously against the external world, non-kin associations are fewer" (Kottak 1990:166). As we have seen, Brazilians are far more likely than Americans to live near family members and see them often. Given this emphasis on family, getting together with relative strangers to talk about gardening or great books or to plan a bake sale strikes Brazilians as odd indeed.

All of these considerations aside, in the end most Brazilians gave a simple down-to-earth explanation when queried about the lack of community élan. They and most of their fellow immigrants, they told me, were in New York for only one reason: to make as much money as fast as possible and return to Brazil. As such, immigrants do not anticipate being in the United States long enough to justify putting their scant time and energy into local groups of any kind. Moreover, to join a club or an organization might be a sign of permanence, evidence that they were really intending to stay in the United States, a proposition that many Brazilians reject. One Brazilian put it in no uncertain terms: "We don't have an immigrant spirit because we are *not* immigrants." Not seeing themselves as immigrants, Brazilians do not identify with other immigrants. Cristina Martes, who studied Brazilians in Boston, notes that "Brazilians don't identify with immigrants because, among other things, they see themselves in a condition of temporary workers . . . whose objective is to make as much money in the United States as possible in order to return to Brazil" (1995:66).

Moreover, despite the ringing charges that Brazilians make against each other, many immigrants acknowledge the help they receive from their compatriots and recognize that the strident discourse about a community on the brink of implosion is overstated. Nearly all of the Brazilian immigrants I talked with said they had gotten their start in the city with the assistance of Brazilian friends or relatives; two-thirds had help finding a place to live and about half that number found jobs through their fellow co-ethnics. Even long after they come to New York, immigrant employment networks continue to function. They help Brazilians who lost jobs find other work or get new jobs with better wages or working conditions.

Brazilians rely on each other for play as much as for work. Parties, gatherings of friends, sports events, or an evening out at a restaurant or club are typically all-Brazilian affairs. And evidence of at least sporadic community solidarity can be found in the tens of thousands of Brazilians from all over the northeastern United States who attend the annual Brazilian Independence Day Fair in early September in Manhattan's Little Brazil.[5] Then, too, whenever a Brazilian singer or musician or dance troupe plays in a New York club or gives a concert, there is invariably a large contingent of Brazilians in the audience noisily celebrating their ethnicity.

Having Faith

A vibrant exception to the paucity of institutional structures in New York's Brazilian immigrant community is found in its churches. This is true in other centers of Brazilian immigration as well. One researcher in Boston found that the only institution that united Brazilians in that city were its ethnic churches, and several dozen churches with services in Portuguese minister to the spiritual needs of Brazilian immigrants in south Florida as well (Badgley 1994; Alves and Ribeiro 2002).

In New York City, churches with religious services in Portuguese— most led by Brazilian clerics—are well attended by the Brazilian faithful. Catholic mass is celebrated in Portuguese at churches in Manhattan and Queens. There are also Baptist and Seventh Day Adventist churches that meet the spiritual needs of Brazilians in the city, along with several Pentecostal churches; the number is uncertain since this denomination has been growing rapidly, opening new churches to accommodate converts in the immigrant community. Rounding out the religious mix are a Spiritist center; several local branches of the Universal Church of the Kingdom of God (*Igreja Universal do Reino de Dios*), a creed founded in Brazil in the late 1970s; Candomblé, a syncretic Afro-Brazilian religion; and Seicho-No-Ié, a sect imported to Brazil from Japan.

A little more than half of the Brazilian immigrants in my study attended religious services with some regularity and their doctrinal loyalties were similar to those found in Brazil. Nearly 75 percent were Catholic, 13 percent were *crentes* ("believers"), as Protestants are called in Brazil, and the rest were either unaffiliated or espoused other beliefs, including Spiritism. Just as in Brazil, membership in evangelical churches has been growing among Brazilians in New York. Estimates suggest that the number of Protestants in Brazil increased fourfold between 1960 and 1990, with the greatest growth in evangelical churches such as the Assembly of God (Mariz 1994). Nevertheless, despite the evangelical upsurge, the majority of Brazilians remain at least nominally Catholic, as do most Brazilian immigrants in New York City.

Prior to the late 1980s no Catholic Church in New York celebrated mass in Portuguese, but reflecting the city's growing Brazilian population, at least three churches in the city now minister to the needs of Brazilian Catholics. The establishment of the city's first mass for Portuguese-speakers at the Church of Our Lady of Perpetual Aid (*Nossa Senhora do Perpetuo Socorro*) in 1990 reflects the changing ethnic composition of New York's immigrant population. For well over a half century, Our Lady of Perpetual Aid had been a Czechoslovakian national parish, but as the descendants of the original Czech congregants moved out to the suburbs, attendance at mass declined sharply and the Archdiocese of New York considered closing the church for good. Learning of this, a longtime Brazilian resident of the city began lobbying local Catholic authorities to institute a Portuguese mass, suggesting that with its dwindling congregation, Our Lady of Perpetual Aid would be a suitable site for such a service. Officials of the archdiocese then contacted the Brazilian consulate in the early 1990s to inquire about the number of Brazilians living in the New York area. "About 60,000," they were told. Impressed by such a critical mass of potential churchgoers, New York's archdiocese endorsed Portuguese-language services for the Brazilian faithful.

While New York is home to a growing community of Brazilian Catholics, it is also the site of a burgeoning number of evangelical churches with services in Portuguese, churches that the late Pope John Paul II once referred to as "the invasion of the sects" (Mariz 1994). Brazilian evangelicals have indeed become increasingly visible in the city's Brazilian community. For the first time in the mid-1990s at the Brazilian Independence Day Street Fair, a contingent of well over one hundred Brazilians—mostly young people—carried "Jesus Saves" signs and distributed literature for the Missionary Christian Church (*Igreja Missionaria Cristiana*), an evangelical denomination in Queens. Ever since, the adherents of one evangelical church or another have been much in evidence at the fair, fervently proclaiming their faith, handing out literature, and proselytizing the swarms of Brazilians from all over the northeastern United States who descend on New York for this annual celebration of ethnicity.

The growth of evangelical churches also has been noted by other observers of the Brazilian immigrant scene. Cristina Martes (1996) suggests that their appeal lies in a theology that exhorts work, applauds personal success, and encourages economic mobility, doctrines that reinforce the predilections of most new immigrants. Moreover, Brazilian Pentecostal churches in Boston, she points out, provide for the material as well as the spiritual needs of their congregants. Their pastors often become involved in the lives of their immigrant disciples, giving them advice on immigration and employment problems, while the churches provide day care, free English classes, donated clothes, and help finding jobs. According to Martes, "The manner in which the Protestant churches become the primordial locus of immigrant sociability is important to an understanding of the success of these churches among Brazilian immigrants, the vast majority of whom were Catholic before they emigrated" (1996:45).

Evangelical churches can be compared to spiritual cocoons, sanctuaries composed of like-minded believers bound together by common moral codes and religious beliefs. These cocoons both sustain and help separate adherents from the alien and sometimes hostile world that surrounds those new to this country. The churches empower their followers by promising them not only a felicitous afterlife but a bountiful one in the here and now. As such, Pentecostalism may be interpreted as less an escape from the temporal world than as a pragmatic strategy for survival in it.

Particularly after September 11, 2001, churches in some Brazilian communities, including those in south Florida and Atlanta, Georgia, have become refuges for undocumented Brazilians fearing arrest and deportation. It is the one place where they feel safe, or as one churchgoer put it, "The church is like my mother's home" (*A igreja é como a casa de minha mãe*) (Vasquez, Ribeiro, and Alves 2008).

The encompassing spirituality of evangelical churchgoers is evident in New York's Brazilian community. Take the Pentecostal Church (Igreja Pentecostal) in Brooklyn as a case in point. Although nearly all of its members reside in Queens, several times a week they make the long trek by subway to Brooklyn to attend the church's Portuguese language services, Bible study classes, and youth fellowship meetings. Once there, they are surrounded by a bevy of like-minded immigrants.

During services the Brazilian pastor exhorts the faithful to abjure drinking alcohol and smoking cigarettes, avoid dancing and secular music, remain pure, if single, and faithful, if married. Girls and women are instructed to dress modestly. Church members are urged to socialize only with each other within a spiritual community, at services held in church and in private homes, at church dinners and other church-sponsored events. Communal outings to the beach in summer were designed to help church members keep their distance from other Brazilians—Brazilians who do not adhere to Pentecostalism's strict precepts on smoking, drinking, modest dress, and behavior.

While members of this congregation are told to avoid nonobservant Brazilians, they are actively engaged with fellow believers, expressing pride in the assistance they give one another in finding jobs and providing food, shelter, and financial aid in times of need. They made a point of telling me how different they were in this regard from their secular compatriots. As one churchgoer put it, "They say we Brazilians are not united, that we don't help each other. But you can see for yourself that's not true here!"

Another determinedly evangelical church—and one of Brazilian origin—is the immodestly named Universal Church (Igreja Universal), which now has an estimated 6 million members in 172 countries including followers in 11 "temples" in New York City and another 10 in the greater New York metropolitan area. In its stress on success, particularly financial success, the theology of the Universal Church is similar to that of some other evangelical ministries. Followers are encouraged to give 10 percent of their earnings to the church and are promised blessings, both monetary and otherwise. "Offerings [to God] are investments," says Bishop Edir Macedo, the Brazilian founder of the church (quoted in *The Economist* 2008:31).

According to one of the church's pastors who is based in New York, the church does not "promise salvation only after death, but we believe God also helps converts in this life. We have many testimonies of people who have prospered and whose prayers have been answered after joining the church." The church has been called "a spiritual version of Wall Street—give up some of your money in hopes of getting a lot more back" (Alvarez, Italiano, and Riberio 2000). And, indeed, prayers for better jobs and improved financial opportunities were the focal point of the service I attended. Much of the sermon was a plea to help raise thousands of dollars for the church's then half completed branch in Brooklyn.[6]

Although its first New York outpost opened in 1986—a time when Brazilian immigrants began flocking to the city—the Universal Church has never focused on ministering to the local Brazilian expatriate community. In fact, its services are conducted in English or Spanish, not in Portuguese, and its cable TV program features Brazilian pastors preaching in "Portanhol," the fractured Spanish often spoken by native speakers of Portuguese.

The abiding goal of the Universal Church is to convert immigrants, but immigrants of all nationalities, not just those from Brazil. Brazilians, in fact, account for less than 20 percent of its New York congregants, and the services I attended were heavily peppered with immigrants from the Caribbean and Central America, with just a handful of Brazilians among them. Branches of the church were established in New York because, said the local pastor, it is a "crossroads drawing people from all over the world and we hope that the church's converts there will start new congregations when they go back to their own countries." In essence, immigrant believers are potential seeds who, it is hoped, will plant the church's teachings in their homelands. Through this process, the church is trying to replicate the enormous success it has had in Brazil, where over eight hundred branches have been established since its founding in 1977. Indeed, the Universal Church, which has been dubbed "the multinational of faith" and the "fast food of faith" now has outposts on all continents (*Veja* 1995a). In a real sense, then, the Universal Church is a transnational church, one that seems well positioned to benefit from the permeability of international borders.

Time Off

While a few Brazilian immigrants, especially evangelicals, spend a good deal of time in church-related activities even during their early months in New York, most new immigrants' single-minded pursuit of the "little green things" leaves them precious little time for anything else. Leisure is not only a rare commodity among immigrants new to this country but, as Brazilians put it, "leisure costs a lot around here." Going out to a restaurant, the movies, or a concert is expensive in a city like New York and leisure also can have hidden costs if it takes time away from work.

Still, as the months go by and Brazilians grow weary of their endless labors, guilt about not spending all their waking hours at work begins to ebb and every last dollar earned is no longer strictly earmarked for that condo in Rio de Janeiro or the small business in Minas Gerais. The gradual process by which immigrants start to think more about life in the host country and less about returning home has been described before (Piore 1979). As this new perspective slowly takes hold, many immigrants become less willing to spend countless hours slaving away at dead-end jobs and more loath to put in overtime or continue to hold down a second job. Working shorter hours means they earn less money, but they spend a little more of it on leisure. Then the suggestions begin: "Let's go out to dinner" or "Why don't we get tickets to the Nascimento concert"[7] or "How about having some of our friends over for a party."

Nevertheless, even when they mellow somewhat and allow themselves a little more time for play, immigrants say that the long hours they continue to put in on the job mean that their social life in New York is a pale reflection of what it was in Brazil. *Cariocas* (natives of Rio de Janeiro) fondly recall the idyllic hours they used to spend drinking icy mugs of *chopp* (draft beer) at beachfront cafés; *mineiros* (natives of Minas Gerais) reminisce about tranquil family picnics in the countryside; and *paulistas* (natives of São Paulo) recount tales of leisurely dinners with friends at one of that city's lively *churrascarias* (barbecue restaurants).

Immigrant social life in New York is a truncated version of what it was in Brazil because it is the rare Brazilian who totally abandons the idea of saving money for the eventual return home. Brazilians are far more likely to spend a quiet evening entertaining family and friends at home than going out for an expensive "night on the town." While half of the Brazilians I interviewed said that they ate out at New York restaurants at least occasionally, only one-third had attended a concert (other than a free one) in the city, and less than one-fifth had ever been to a nightclub.

When they do go out, Brazilians tend to patronize restaurants and clubs that feature the food and music of their homeland. By 2008, New York City had two dozen such establishments with several more in nearby suburbs. Immigrants generally avoid the tourist-oriented Brazilian restaurants in the vicinity of Manhattan's Little Brazil, preferring the less costly ones in Queens and Newark. A Brazilian-style *churrascaria a rodizio* (literally, barbecue in the round) in Queens, where waiters pass from table to table with large skewers of grilled beef, pork, and chicken, is particularly popular with immigrants. The appeal of this cavernous eatery, which serves gargantuan amounts of food at reasonable prices, extends well beyond the Brazilian community; its diners mirror the striking ethnic rainbow of immigrant New York.

Aside from eating out, some immigrants also spend their hard-earned dollars for concerts and shows with Brazilian artists. In the last several years many of that nation's best-known entertainers—Caetano Veloso, Gal Costa, Milton Nascimento, Gilberto Gil, Maria Bethania, Beth Carvalho, Ivan Lins—have given concerts in the city or have appeared in New York clubs. And when Brazilian singers or musicians are featured in free open-air performances such as Summerstage in Central Park, the extent and verve of the city's Brazilian population becomes apparent. Hordes of Brazilian immigrants inevitably turn out to sing and shout and dance to the music and cheer on their compatriots in joyous observance of their common roots.

Warm weather means outings to one of the metropolitan area's beaches as well as get-togethers for cookouts and picnics in urban parks. Excursions to the seashore in summer are especially popular among *cariocas* who pine for Rio's famed beaches. Brazilians say they can always spot knots of their compatriots at the seashore because Brazilian women are the only ones clad in *tangas*, the tiny string bikinis manufactured in Brazil that have become a ubiquitous symbol of Rio de Janeiro and its "Girl from Ipanema."

While Brazilians go to the beach or city parks or occasionally dine out or go to shows, informal gatherings at home are by far the most common modes of social interaction in the immigrant community. Indeed, some Brazilians get together with the same group of friends week in and week out. They might drink *caipirinhas* or beer or have a *feijoada*, or perhaps watch the latest installment of a Brazilian *telenovela* (soap opera) on TV Globo, or roll up the rug and do the *samba*.[8] Parties are also given to mark special occasions in the lives of immigrants, to celebrate a birth or marriage, for example, or to bid a boisterous farewell to a compatriot returning to Brazil.

Futebol (soccer)—that quintessential Brazilian sport—is also a favored pastime in the community. Almost a quarter of the Brazilian men in my study played *futebol* at least occasionally, although only about one in ten were members of organized soccer teams. Some of the teams have regularly scheduled games, say every Saturday morning weather permitting, but others play only sporadically. The soccer teams are either all-Brazilian affairs, like the Athletic Club of Minas Gerais, or of mixed nationality. The relatively modest numbers involved in soccer teams belie the singular role that *futebol* plays in the Brazilian community both as a major spectator sport and a signature of shared identity. Many immigrants of all ages and both sexes regularly attend soccer games played by their compatriots. For example, on Memorial and Labor Day weekends several hundred Brazilians cheer from the sidelines as Brazilian soccer teams compete at an outdoor playing field in Manhattan. These sporting events have a distinctly Brazilian flair. Spectators are dressed in green and gold—Brazil's national colors—Brazilian flags flutter in the wind, and street vendors sell *salgadinhos* and *guaraná*, Brazilian snacks and soft drinks.

The true significance of this sport as a symbol of Brazilian national identity was only brought home to me when the World Cup games in soccer were played in the United States in the summer of 1994. American newspaper and TV commentators often noted the heady exuberance of Brazilian fans, immigrants and visitors alike, as Brazil became the first nation ever to win its fourth World Cup. They were *tetracampeões*, "four-time champions" headlined the sport's page of the *New York Times*. From New York to California—in what was typically the first media coverage ever of Brazilian immigrants in this country—accounts of carnival-like street parades and crowds of wildly enthusiastic fans made the news. In northern California, for example, where Brazil's winning team played most of its games, the local news media suddenly discovered San Francisco's large Brazilian community (Ribeiro 1999).

All over the United States in cities with sizeable Brazilian populations, Brazilians celebrated their victory with vivacious abandon (Longman 1994). In Washington, D.C., after Brazil beat the Netherlands in the quarter finals, the Brazilian crowd that had been jammed into a local Brazilian restaurant to watch the game on a big screen TV spilled out into the street, dancing the *samba* and blocking traffic as dozens of their compatriots drove by, horns honking and cars festooned with Brazilian flags. In New York's Little Brazil, before the start of the final game, throngs of Brazilian fans milled about. A large TV screen had been placed curbside in front of a store selling Brazilian products and street vendors hawked beer and soft drinks. Within a half hour of Brazil's World Cup triumph over Italy, hordes of Brazilians arriving from Queens poured out of subway stations to join the raucous open-air celebration already in progress. Groups playing *batucada*, Afro-Brazilian percussion music, shared the packed street with lines of *samba* dancers, some in very skimpy attire indeed. There were also people wrapped in large Brazilian flags wearing extravagant green and yellow wigs, a man walking on stilts, and several garishly dressed Brazilian drag queens. A line of New York police officers stood by with a dazed look in their eyes, scratching their heads as if to say, "What's going on here? Who are these people and where did they come from?"—evidence of the ongoing invisibility of this immigrant community, a topic to which I now turn.

Ethnicity, Race, and Gender

The police officers on duty at the celebration of Brazil's World Cup victory are not the only New Yorkers unaware of this new immigrant stream. Theirs is a "secret, silent migration," as one Brazilian put it, since few people outside their own community are aware of it. Brazilians are truly an invisible minority because of Americans' confusion about who they are and what language they speak. Moreover, Little Brazil Street notwithstanding, Brazilian invisibility also results from the lack of a tangible community in the city, a locale tinged with its own distinct ethnicity like Chinatown or Little Italy, or even a residential neighborhood Brazilians could call their own. Nor is it a surprise that hardly any New Yorkers are aware of Little Brazil's existence since the few Brazilian enterprises on this Manhattan street are interspersed with restaurants and businesses of many nationalities, muting the Brazilian presence there.

Brazilians are also unknown to most New Yorkers because they have received very little news coverage. The first mention of the city's Brazilian community in the *New York Times*, for example, was in an article on the sport's page about the noisy enthusiasm of local Brazilian fans during the World Cup games (Longman 1994). Another news item about Brazilian immigrants was published a year later when the murder of a Brazilian jogger in Central Park made the front page and the paper did a brief background story on the community entitled "Slaying Shocks Usually Upbeat Brazilians" (Lee 1995). In fact, it was not until 2005 that the *New York Times* ran a story about the growing Brazilian presence in Queens and another one acknowledging the growing number of Brazilians in the United States and the fact that many had arrived illegally by crossing the border from Mexico (Berger and Santos 2005; Rohter 2005).[1]

Brazilians are also absent from media coverage of the new immigrant groups that are making New York's ethnic and linguistic mosaic ever more complex. For example, when the Ellis Island Museum in New York's harbor opened, the city's role as the premiere immigrant gateway to this country was highlighted and the New York media ran stories about many of the city's recent immigrant groups. A one-hour prime-time TV special covered the new wave of migration and featured clips or mentioned immigrants from at least fifteen countries, but not Brazil. Likewise, in a magazine cover story about the intricate medley of ethnic groups that comprise New York, thirty-two different nationalities were cited, including Argentines, Cambodians, Thais, Guatemalans, Trinidadians, and "40 or 50 Laotian families living in the Bronx." Brazilians were not in the mix (Brenner 1991).

What is all the more surprising about the ongoing invisibility of this burgeoning ethnic colony is that it is unaffected by the popularity of all things Brazilian. Over the last two decades clubs featuring Brazilian music or performers or concerts with Brazilian musicians have become a staple of New York night life. Trendy restaurants featuring both real and faux Brazilian cuisine, while not quite legion, are very popular. Brazil was even called "the nation *du jour* among New York style-setters" by *New York Magazine*. This is why Brazilian food and music have received abundant coverage in the pages of the *New York Times* and other media outlets. But this interest and exposure has rarely been extended to the Brazilian immigrant community itself. Part of the explanation lies in Americans' ignorance about their "southern neighbors," most especially Brazil. But it also rests on Brazilian ethnicity as a contested category.

American Ignorance

In the United States, Latin America is often portrayed as "just one civilization artificially divided into different countries," or, as President Ronald Reagan said upon returning from a trip to Latin America in the early 1980s, "You'd be surprised. They're all individual countries" (Sims 1995:4E). The vast majority of Americans, even educated ones, have no idea that Brazil is in any way different from the rest of Latin America. For example, after consulting with a physician in New York City—a highly trained specialist in his field—on a minor medical matter, I mentioned that I was going to Brazil to teach for a semester at a university in Rio de Janeiro. "Oh," he said, "you must be very fluent in Spanish." "No, actually, I am not," I replied. "But I do speak Portuguese." This illustrates the problem. Despite the size of Brazil (about 190 million people) and its importance (the ninth largest economy in the world), most Americans know very little about Brazil, including the fact that Brazilians speak Portuguese.

A professor at an elite New England college found from surveys he gave to students in his Latin American history class that less than 60 percent of them knew that Brazilians speak Portuguese; the rest thought that Spanish is the language of Brazil and that Portuguese is spoken only in Portugal (Davis 1997b). Similarly, a survey commissioned by the Brazilian embassy in Washington, D.C. in 2000 measured Americans' knowledge (or lack thereof) of Brazilian culture and geography. Of the one thousand Americans included in the survey, 39 percent claimed that the official language of Brazil is Spanish and 23 percent claimed that the capital of Brazil is Buenos Aires; barely 19 percent knew that Brazil's capital is Brasília (http://www.jornal.atarde.com.br).

American confusion about Brazilian language and ethnicity dates back decades, at least to the era of the "Brazilian bombshell" Carmen Miranda, who, at one point during the 1940s, was the highest paid movie actress in the United States. Her elaborate kitsch costumes with their flouncy skirts and bare midriff topped off by a monumental fruit-laden headdress and her exaggerated accent helped shape American perceptions of Brazil and Brazilians. Carmen Miranda became the generic "Latina" whose movies were set indistinguishably in Cuba and Mexico as well as in Brazil. She represented an undifferentiated "south of the border" reality to many Americans (Davis 1997a).

The contemporary depiction of Brazil by the U.S. entertainment industry certainly does nothing to educate Americans about that land. A case in point is an episode from 2002 of *The Simpsons*, TV's favorite dysfunctional family. When the Simpsons visit Rio de Janeiro they find bloodthirsty monkeys roaming Copacabana Beach and rats threatening pedestrians. Tourists are kidnapped by taxi drivers, mugged by children, and sexually harassed by police. Then when the family visits a *samba* school to learn the *macarena*—a Latino specialty not performed in Brazil—the teacher shows them the "penetrada," a fictitious, lascivious dance. The episode so offended city fathers that they threatened to sue the producers of the show for damage to Rio's international image and loss of tourist revenue. Then Brazilian President Fernando Henrique Cardoso entered the fray, claiming that the cartoon "brought a distorted vision of Brazilian reality" (Bellos 2002).

Brazilian immigrants decry such American ignorance of their land and language. As one immigrant put it: "Americans have very little culture when it comes to Latin America." Stories about American naiveté are legion in New York's Brazilian community and were recounted to me with a mixture of hilarity and chagrin. A popular one concerned the benighted American who telephoned the Brazilian consulate in search of tourist information about Buenos Aires. Another was about the American who asked a Brazilian immigrant, "Just what kind of Spanish do you speak?" After she replied that she was from Brazil and did *not* speak Spanish, the American said, "Oh, of course, you're from Brazil. That's the country where the upper class speaks Portuguese and the lower class speaks Spanish." As one Brazilian who was barely able to contain his frustration put it, "There are 300 million Portuguese-speakers in the world today and I find it just incredible that Americans don't know there is a difference between our language and Spanish." In fact, more people speak Portuguese as their native language than French, German, Italian, or Japanese (Rohter 2006).

Brazilians told other tales of the American penchant for reducing the rich complexity that is Brazil to a simplistic duality. In the American imagination, Brazil is typecast in one of two ways. It is either the land of white, sparkling beaches—the stereotype of the "Girl from Ipanema," of sultry mulattos, of string bikinis, of *sambas*—or the home of the vast impenetrable Amazon—the cliché of the lush, primeval, tropical forest. The latter image is evident in the following anecdotes. An immigrant from São Paulo, a modern metropolis of some 16 million people, was questioned about the "Indians roaming" the streets of his city. Another Brazilian said that Americans regularly asked her inane questions like, "Do you eat snakes?" and "Do you have windows in your houses?" Americans, she said, "think we live in huts. It's disappointing because I thought Americans were so cultured and they don't even know where Brazil is!" One Brazilian expressed annoyance that many U.S. Hispanics are also ignorant about Brazil and cited a Spanish-language publication that had returned the capital of Brazil to Rio de Janeiro—Brasília has been the capital for nearly fifty years. There was also the following exchange between President George W. Bush and President Fernando Henrique Cardoso of Brazil, as reported in the on-line edition of the German magazine *Der Spiegel*: "'Are there Blacks in Brazil? Do you have Blacks too?' Bush asked the astonished Brazilian president. Bush's [then] national security advisor, Condoleezza Rice, came to the rescue. Noticing how stunned Cardoso was, Dr. Rice quickly said, 'Mr. President, Brazil has probably more Blacks than the USA. It is the country with the most Blacks outside of Africa.'" The Brazilian president later diplomatically remarked that Bush was "still in training on South America."

What *Is* a Brazilian?

Among newly arrived Brazilian immigrants in the United States, American ignorance of Brazil and American ethnic categories both contribute to a new consciousness of what it means to be Brazilian. They also present Brazilians with a dilemma, as in the following case: On most U.S. employment forms, job applicants are asked to indicate their race and ethnic group. A typical category is: "Hispanic from Mexico, Central America, or South America." Even though Brazilians are from South America, they cannot check this category because they are not Hispanic since the term refers to Spanish-speakers or those of Spanish-speaking descent and, as we know, Brazilians speak Portuguese. So Brazilians are South Americans; they are also Latin Americans (Latinos), but they are *not* Hispanics.[2] In fact, it has been shown that their national identity—Brazilian—is their primary social identity (Martes 2007).

Like some other immigrant groups in the United States, Brazilians contest or at least sidestep American racial and ethnic categorizations (Basch, Glick Schiller, and Szanton Blanc 1994). One of the first things that Brazilian immigrants learn to say after they arrive in New York is: "We are *not* Hispanic and we don't speak Spanish!" There are several reasons why Brazilian immigrants strongly object to being labeled Hispanic. Brazilians try to distinguish themselves linguistically and culturally from other Latin American immigrant groups in New York partly because of cultural pride, what they see as the uniqueness of their "race" (*raça*). This attitude, in turn, has deep roots in Brazil, a nation with a keen sense of its own distinctiveness from the rest of the continent. Brazilians have long been indifferent to other Latin American nations, dismissing their common Iberian heritage as of little importance. As such, Brazilians lack a common identity either with other South Americans or with Hispanics in general. In fact, the term "Hispanic" (*hispano*) does not even exist in Brazil. There "Spanish" refers to people from Spain, while citizens of Spanish-speaking countries in Latin America are called Mexicans, Chileans, Peruvians, Argentines, and so on.

Most Brazilians believe that Americans treat them better when they make it clear that they are *not* Hispanic. They insist that Hispanics are discriminated against in the United States and that when Americans confuse them with Hispanics, they too suffer from anti-Hispanic bias.

Brazilians' efforts to disassociate themselves from Hispanics also grow out of their own prejudice and feelings of superiority over the city's other Latin American immigrant groups. Said one Brazilian in comparing his compatriots favorably to Hispanics, "Everybody knows Rio de Janeiro! The Hispanic has nothing. What city will he talk about that is universally known?" (quoted in Marcus 2008:282).

Such attitudes are rooted in the comparatively elite social status of Brazilian immigrants. Since the vast majority of Brazilians in New York are from the middle strata of Brazilian society and many are well educated, they consider it an insult to be confused with the rest of the city's Latino population, a large portion of which is poorer and has less education than they do. A few Brazilians even object to being called "Latino," although it is an accurate designation since it refers to individuals from Latin America without reference to the language they speak. Nevertheless, some Brazilians dislike the term because they believe it carries the dual stigmas of prejudice and low socioeconomic status (Martes 2007).

As such, issues of social class and prejudice coalesce in the construction of identity among Brazilians living abroad, an identity that is built, in part, on what I call a "we're not like them" perspective. I first noticed this among Brazilians in New York City and it has also been observed by researchers studying Brazilian populations in Boston and south Florida (Margolis 2007; Sales 1998, 1999, 2003; Fleischer 2002; Resende 2002, 2005).

A "we're not like them" outlook is evident in a study of Brazilian housecleaners in Boston, which found that Brazilians highlight their ethnic identity by praising their own work ethic and comparing it favorably to that of Hispanic women doing the same job (Fleischer 2002). Brazilians, they say, are harder working, more thorough, and more reliable than Hispanic housekeepers. By being extremely fastidious, Brazilian housecleaners attempt to undercut the "cultural misunderstanding" common among Americans that all housecleaners are simple, uneducated, lower-class people.

The antipathy toward being identified with other Latin Americans is not limited to Brazilians in the United States. In similar fashion, Brazilians of Japanese descent who have immigrated to Japan take offense at being confused with Peruvians of Japanese descent living there and assume an air of superiority to immigrants of Japanese heritage from other Latin American nations.[3] "The Peruvian is lazy," opined a Japanese-Brazilian. "I detest being called *nambeijin* (South American) by the Japanese because I don't want to be put in the same group as the Peruvians and Argentines" (quoted in Chigusa 1994:48).

There is one final twist to this complex pirouette of ethnic identity. While many Brazilian immigrants in New York are angered when they are confused with Hispanics, glorying in their cultural and linguistic distinctiveness, a few Brazilians—usually those who have been in this country for several years—do not want to be identified with their own compatriots either. These are the same immigrants who talk about avoiding other Brazilians and spurning them as friends, part of the "you can't trust Brazilians in the United States" discourse that was discussed in the last chapter. One researcher has labeled this the "Brazilian paradox" (Badgley 1994), the regrettable situation in which Brazilians insist on maintaining their separateness from other ethnic groups, while also remaining emotionally distant from one another.

They Were Not Counted

The undercount of Brazilians in the U.S. censuses of 1990 and 2000 is one practical consequence of their enigmatic ethnicity. Only a fraction of Brazilians were counted or, if they were counted, their nationality was not specified. The actual number of Brazilians living in New York City and elsewhere in the United States who were missed in the census enumerations is unknown, but, as we have seen, the undercount in both 1990 and 2000 may have been as high as 80 percent for the country as a whole.

The undercount of Brazilians is a direct outgrowth of the census categories used. "Brazil" does not appear on the census form even though nearly every other country in Latin America is listed. Citizens from one of the few countries not named can check the box marked "Yes, other Spanish/Hispanic" and fill in the blank with their country of origin. But, as we know, Brazilians are not Hispanics and they vehemently reject being designated as such. Many Brazilians who were willing to fill out the census forms did not do so because of the limitations of the ethnic categories provided. For the first time the 2000 census used the term "Hispanic/Latino" with Latino being defined in the same way as Hispanic—Spanish-speaking or of Spanish origin or descent. However, also for the first time, this categorization *specifically* excluded Brazilians and Brazilians who checked Hispanic/Latino and wrote in "Brazilian" were marked "not Hispanic/Latino" and their nationality went unrecorded (Marrow 2002).

Restrictive ethnic categories were not the only reason many Brazilians did not participate in the two federal censuses. Fear also played a part. Many undocumented Brazilians were afraid to fill out the forms because they did not believe that census information was confidential and felt certain that it would be turned over to immigration authorities. Apathy was more important still. A number of Brazilian immigrants told me that they and their compatriots did not send in the forms because "we couldn't care less about the census." After all, they reminded me, most Brazilians are in the United States only for the short-term and have no interest in being counted (Margolis 1995a).

The Color Spectrum

Brazilian immigrants in New York often talk about being confused with Hispanics and about the peculiarity of American ethnic designations. They also discuss many other issues that touch on their identity in the United States: their invisibility as a distinct ethnic group, the lack of unity among their fellow Brazilians, and the social class and education of their immigrant compatriots. But, I rarely heard them discuss a related subject: race and race relations within the Brazilian community.

We already know that the racial make-up of the Brazilian immigrant population in New York is weighted toward the lighter end of the color spectrum, making it atypical of Brazil as a nation. Recall that 80 percent of the Brazilians in my study were white, 8 percent were light mulatto or mulatto, and 8 percent were black. In all, people of color appeared to account for only about 16 percent of New York's Brazilian community, a far cry from the nearly 45 percent reported in the Brazilian census of 2000 for the population as a whole (Fundação Instituto Brasileiro de Geografia e Estatística 2000).

The racial composition of New York's Brazilian population was corroborated both by Brazilian immigrants themselves and by my own observations at many large gatherings of Brazilians—street fairs, sports events, concerts, and the like—during the course of my field research. Brazilians of color, including blacks and mulattos, typically comprised 10 percent or less of those in attendance.

Ironically, although Brazilians of color are underrepresented in New York's immigrant population, white Brazilians seem to interact more with their black and mulatto compatriots in the United States than they do in Brazil (Ehrlich 1990). This is not as contradictory as it appears, however, because social interaction in Brazil is generally influenced more by social class than by race. In other words, Brazilians of similar socioeconomic status tend to socialize with each other and since Brazilians in New York, including Brazilians of color, are mostly from the middle strata of Brazilian society, white middle-class immigrants are more likely to have contact with their black and brown brothers and sisters in New York than they are in Brazil.

The greater social interaction between Brazilians of all racial hues in New York helps reduce the heavy baggage of racial stereotyping that some white Brazilians bring with them to this country. That white Brazilians are more likely to see people of color in middle-class positions in the United

States than they did in Brazil also plays a role in reducing prejudice. Said one immigrant: "I think that racial attitudes towards blacks change for all Brazilians who come to the United States. In Brazil you don't see [blacks eating] in restaurants, and here you do. At the beginning it's difficult to accept this idea because we are not accustomed to this. We grew up in a society that has more blacks than whites, but blacks have always lived under very bad conditions in Brazil. What changed was my perception of the Negro race. I respect them for what they've achieved here" (quoted in Ehrlich 1989:62).

When Brazilian immigrants talk about race, one common element in their discourse is how "different" African Americans are from people of color in Brazil. White Brazilians contrast what they perceive as the "aggressiveness" of Afro-Americans with the submissive behavior they had come to expect from Afro-Brazilians back home (Marcus 2008). But they are confusing race and class. In Brazil, people from the lower echelons of society are expected to act with deference and respect toward those higher on the social ladder. Because Afro-Brazilians are disproportionately found in the lower strata of Brazilian society, Brazilians conflate such behavior with skin color and are "surprised" when African Americans do not behave in a similarly deferential manner.

Gender Snapshots

Like racial stereotypes, gender role traditions also soften under the sway of international migration. To cite one pertinent example: although women are traditionally seen as migrating for family reasons—to join a male breadwinner or to reunite the family—my own and other research challenges this common notion (Simon and DeLey 1986; Zentgraf 1995). Less than one-third of the Brazilian women I studied were married at the time I interviewed them, and even fewer were married when they first arrived in the United States. In other words, contrary to conventional wisdom, family considerations did not spur most of these women to migrate to the United States. In fact, I found that Brazilian women came to New York for exactly the same reason that Brazilian men did—to take jobs that paid far more than any they could ever find back home (Galvão 2005).[4]

When women migrate abroad to seek work, gendered labor recruitment is often involved. That is, the particular labor market needs of specific cities in the United States or other host countries may select for female (or male) migrants (Repak 1995). For example, male immigrants might readily find employment in a certain locale if workers for low-wage construction jobs were in demand there. Domestic service is another case of gendered labor recruitment since the call for live-in housekeepers, day maids, nannies, and babysitters is almost entirely a demand for *female* labor.

Employment in this sector of the labor market may have given immigrant women an advantage of sorts. Since 1986 when the U.S. Congress passed the Immigration Reform and Control Act, which tightened penalties on employers who hire undocumented workers, immigrant women have been able to find work somewhat more easily than immigrant men. The reason is that employers of babysitters, housekeepers, and nannies are less likely than others to ask about their employee's legal status or to require that they have a green card (Repak 1995).

New Land, New Roles

Whether they work as nannies, maids, street vendors, or go-go dancers, Brazilian women's employment is the primary catalyst for shifts in gender roles. Some of these shifts are problematic given the baggage of traditional Brazilian gender expectations that many immigrants bring with them to the United States. In Brazil when a woman works outside the home, her salary is typically viewed as only supplementing the family budget. The woman is still responsible for domestic tasks and caring for the children. Even in middle-class families who employ servants, it is implicit that household tasks fall under the woman's purview. The man is seen as the family provider and the home is not within his sphere of concern (DeBiaggi 2002).

Crucial to gender adjustments is the earning power of women immigrants in the United States. Women's greater financial autonomy is what sets the stage for a reformulation of traditional Brazilian gender roles. Many immigrant women, particularly married women, contend that their former dependence is replaced by the "executive power" (*poder executivo*) they acquire from their new role as breadwinners. They take jobs and for the first time in their lives they earn as much or even more than their husbands do. As one Brazilian woman put it, "Now the check is in *MY* name!" (quoted in Marcus 2008).

This financial clout gives women more familial decision-making power. A Brazilian husband living in Boston agreed: "Here the woman has much more say than in Brazil because she has money. In Brazil she had to be a good girl and keep quiet. Here everyone says that the husband has to help out" (quoted in DeBiaggi 1996:25). Indeed, I found no evidence that the conventional Brazilian worldview in which the street (*a rua*) is a male preserve and the home (*a casa*) is a female one negated the power bestowed by women's financial contribution to the household (Da Matta 1991).

To be sure, some Brazilian men feel emasculated as a result of their spouses' newly found financial independence and the social freedom that can accompany it. According to one researcher, Brazilian men, in general, have a more difficult time adjusting to the exigencies of the immigrant experience than Brazilian women (Marcus 2008). Men who work in construction jobs in enclosed environments, for example, have less exposure to American culture and less opportunity to practice English than do women who work as housekeepers and who necessarily interact on a daily basis with their employers.

To be sure, Brazilian women are not unique in their newly found independence as international migrants. Other research has cited the effects of paid employment on women's status and role within the context of international migration (Pessar 1985; Haines 1986; Hondagneu-Sotelo 1994; Levitt 2001). A study of migration of Dominicans to New York, for example, noted that since immigrant wages in the city were low—at least in the early years of migration—most Dominican households were incapable of maintaining the traditional division of labor, with men the wage earners and women the dependents. Men's wages simply were insufficient to support a household, making it essential that women contribute to basic living expenses (Grasmuck and Pessar 1992). Similarly, Haitian women who held jobs in New York were found to have far greater economic autonomy than they had back home, particularly women who had not been employed in Haiti or whose earnings only supplemented their husbands' (Buchanan 1979). These studies suggest, then, that a realignment of economic responsibilities can moderate the time-worn patriarchal ideology that asserts that men should be a family's lone or, at least, its primary breadwinner.

But women's greater autonomy within the context of migration sometimes comes at a price. While women's employment lessens dependence on men and may enhance self-confidence, research suggests that women's new financial authority also can lead to greater discord between the sexes, particularly among wives and husbands. Ironically, for some immigrant women the achievement of economic parity has not led to more egalitarian households but to the break up of their marriages (Grasmuck and Pessar 1992). Here is a case in point from my own research on Brazilian immigrants in New York City. It illustrates just how a reordering of traditional roles can transform lives and gender relations. Veronica and Claudio had been married for ten years. They had one son and lived in an apartment in Astoria, Queens. They had been living in New York for two years when I met them, and both had jobs cleaning apartments. Veronica was earning somewhat more than Claudio and she purchased whatever she pleased with her wages—a dining room table, a color TV set—without consulting Claudio. On weekends Veronica often went out with friends to restaurants and nightclubs. Claudio, who preferred to spend his time listening to his large CD collection, stayed home with their son.

This lifestyle contrasted sharply with what they were used to in Brazil. There Claudio was an assistant bank manager as well as the sole family breadwinner. Veronica was a full-time housewife. Having no income of her own, Veronica never made a major purchase without her husband's approval. On weekends Claudio went out with his friends to bars or to the beach, while Veronica stayed home with their young son. She would make dinner and sometimes Claudio came home to eat it; other times he would not.

After several months in New York Veronica was clearly enjoying her heady new financial independence and the partial reversal of her family's traditional division of labor. Claudio was far less pleased. At this point, Veronica began telling Claudio that he was simply "paying for his past sins" in Brazil—not showing up for dinner, going out with his friends, and leaving her at home. As a result of these role shifts, a great deal of friction was evident between the two. They have since divorced and Veronica, who continues to live with their son in Queens, is now married to an American of Puerto Rican ancestry. Claudio has returned to Brazil.

A number of Brazilians told me that this scenario was not uncommon and that many marriages broke up after couples moved to New York. Most credited the break ups to the fact that married women were far more likely to be employed in the United States than they were in Brazil and that with a job came greater economic autonomy and a renegotiation of traditional gender roles. One Brazilian even told a friend who had just arrived in New York that, if he valued his marriage, he should discourage his wife from going to work. He then bet him that they would get divorced if she took a job. She went to work at a restaurant and, indeed, within two months they separated.

This case and that of Veronica and Claudio point to one factor that seems to be critical in a couple's willingness and ability to moderate conventional gender roles: whether or not they married or began living together before or after they came to the United States. Brazilian immigrants suggested that couples who meet in New York and then marry are less likely to wind up separated or divorced than those who were married before leaving Brazil. In New York, the reasoning goes, the woman was already employed when the couple first met, so her work and the economic clout that goes with it was a given from the start of the relationship. This seems to be true of Brazilian immigrants in Boston as well since evidence suggests that divorce rates are higher among couples who immigrated there together. Said one member of Boston's Brazilian immigrant community: "To tell the truth there are many separations between couples here. These couples aren't able to stay together because it is so liberal here. In Brazil, the man works and the woman stays home. It is rare that a woman works. Here a woman has to work just like a man and everything is split up. It seems that people become . . . I don't know . . . selfish. I think that here everyone has equal rights and this brings on many problems" (quoted in Badgley 1994:84–85).

The time and place of marriage also may play a critical role in the explosive issue of the household division of labor—who cleans, who makes dinner and washes the dishes, and who takes care of the kids, if there are any. Social class and education also seem to affect the domestic division of labor. Research suggests that better-educated couples who are both employed come closer to an "egalitarian model of conjugal relations" than do those with less education and a dependent spouse (Safa 1995:46).

The renegotiation of who does what at home can be a volatile question that effects the health and longevity of marital and other intimate relationships. A Brazilian woman said that while her boyfriend "never did anything domestic back in Brazil," he had changed quite a lot since immigrating to the United States and they now had a more equitable division of labor at home. One male immigrant told me of his own updated ideology: "You lose a lot of preconceived notions about the relationship between men and women. Here in the U.S. the man participates more in the life of the house and the woman has much more dialogue with the husband. The man allows [sic] the woman to work out of necessity. A man who helps the woman in domestic chores begins to appreciate what housework is like and he gives it more value."

Once again, studies of other immigrant groups in the United States suggest parallels with the Brazilian case. For example, Salvadoran women in Washington, D.C., who formed attachments to men after migration were somewhat more successful in getting them to participate in domestic work than those whose relationships predated their arrival in this country (Repak

1995). Jamaican men were more likely to "help" their wives with housework and child care in New York than they were back home, and many Jamaican immigrants, both male and female, began questioning "the legitimacy of the traditional division of labor that assigns only women to housework" (Foner 1986:152). And when women from the Dominican Republic who had moved to New York were asked how relations between husbands and wives had improved since leaving home, the response was that a more equitable division of household responsibilities was taking place. For most of these women, in fact, an "improvement in gender relations had been an unintended outcome of the immigrant experience" (Grasmuck and Pessar 1992:155). It is precisely this "improvement" in gender relations that makes some Brazilian immigrant women reluctant to return home. What, they wonder, will become of the greater equality they enjoyed in New York? What will happen to the increased freedom and autonomy that comes with a paycheck once they are back in Brazil?

From Sojourner to Settler

"A person really can be successful in Brazil," opined Pedro, the husband in another popular Brazilian soap opera about emigration called *Patria Minha* (My Homeland), which aired in Brazil in the mid-1990s. Pedro and his wife, Esther, both immigrants in New York, were arguing about their future and whether or not they should return to Brazil. "No, you can't," Esther shot back with some vehemence. "Brazil is corruption, it's hunger, it's . . . I don't know. It's just *not* a place where you can really succeed." Some real-life variation of this fictional conversation doubtless is repeated over and over again in the homes of Brazilian immigrants in New York and elsewhere in the United States.

But the decision of immigrants to stay in this country or return home is not nearly as clear-cut and simple as it may appear. Moreover, even when a decision is "final" it is sometimes reversed. Take the case of Huberto, a Brazilian immigrant who had lived in New York for about five years. After much thought and some uncertainty, he finally decided to give up his apartment and his job managing a popular coffee bar in Manhattan and go home to São Paulo "for good." Yet, less than six weeks after returning to Brazil, Huberto's compatriot and coworker at the coffee bar told me that Huberto had phoned from Brazil to say that he had been unable to find a decent job and was discouraged by the economic situation he found there. As a result, he had already booked a flight and was planning to return to New York in several weeks.

"Our Heads Are in Two Places"

Many factors come into play in the initial resolve to stay in the United States or to go home and the decision is almost never an easy one. The picture is particularly murky for Brazilian immigrants because, unlike some immigrant groups who arrive in the United States determined to make a new life in this country, most Brazilians, at least at first, come here with the sole intention of making a new life *back home*. That is, they are only in New

York or Boston or Miami or Los Angeles to make money for the return to Brazil. Initially, then, Brazilians see themselves as sojourners rather than as settlers. Sojourners maintain their orientation toward their own country; they are little engaged with the host society and they live for the day they can go home (Chavez 1988). Sojourners are literally people between two worlds; they live in a state of "in-betweenness" (Basch, Glick Schiller, Szanton Blanc 1994:8). As Brazilians in New York often put it: "We are here, but our heads [or hearts] are in Brazil." In a real sense, they are torn between their material and emotional needs.

Brazilians, in essence, become transnational migrants, people who sustain familial, cultural, and economic ties that ignore international borders and span the home and the host societies (Basch, Glick Schiller, and Szanton Blanc 1994). The dual orientation of Brazilians and other transnational migrants is partly dependent on modern communication and transportation networks. Rapid transmission of news, sports, and culture via the internet, television, videotape, e-mail, fax, and telephone allows transnational migrants to stay in touch with what is happening back home. Brazilian immigrants in New York, for example, generally know more about news and sports scores in Brazil than in the United States. In fact, they are able to stay remarkably up to date about events in their homeland (Margolis 1995b). Be it the latest soap opera, soccer match, carnival extravaganza, or political scandal, Brazilian immigrants can have immediate access to the event through TV Globo, Brazil's largest television network, which, since 1999, has been widely available via satellite in the United States.

Brazilian immigrants also stay in touch with their homeland through occasional visits there. Whether or not immigrants travel to Brazil themselves depends on how long they have been in the United States and, more importantly, on their legal status. The general rule is that the longer Brazilians have lived in this country, the better the odds that they have a green card, and the more likely they are to have gone back to Brazil to visit. A green card allows an immigrant to come and go from the United States at will as long as the stay abroad is less than one year. Despite the recency of this migration stream and its high percentage of undocumented immigrants, well over half the Brazilians in my study had gone home for a visit at least once since arriving in this country. However, as we will see in the postscript, the relative ease of travel between the United States and Brazil has been considerably restricted since the events of September 11, 2001.

By far the most constant means of contact with relatives and friends back home is via telephone and for those with computers, e-mail. Several immigrants also used camcorders to send videotaped messages to Brazil about their New York activities.[1] Nearly all Brazilians in my study called home on a regular basis and they spent a lot of money to do so. Monthly phone bills of $80 to $150 were common, while a few immigrants sheepishly admitted that their bills reached $200 a month or more. By 2008 Brazilian immigrants were using Skype to speak to friends and relatives in Brazil, or they bought calling cards that allowed them to phone Brazil for as little as 2 cents a minute (Marcus 2008).

Still, in the 1990s AT&T apparently realized what good customers they had in Brazilian immigrants. A "phone home" advertising campaign suggested that "long distance calls to Brazil are easier than a one-note samba," an allusion to the classic Brazilian lyric. Here is an illustration of how readily Brazilians call home: When I was in a home furnishing store in Manhattan and asked the Brazilian owner, a longtime resident of New York City, how to say "wine rack" in Portuguese, he was disturbed when he could not recall the phrase. As quickly as one might consult a dictionary, he dialed Brazil to ask a friend.

Sending money home is another sign of sojourner status as well as a major incentive for transnational migration. Frequent remittances indicate a close association and identification with the home community as well as a higher probability of return. As noted earlier, just over half of the Brazilians in my New York study sent money home. Most immigrants sent remittances to their parents; only about 20 percent sent them to spouses and children. Recall that much of the money sent to Brazil by immigrants was actually for their own future use there. Savings might be earmarked for buying a house or apartment, starting a business, or making a major purchase or investment. For the most part, then, Brazilian immigrants in New York City again do not conform to prevailing stereotypes, that of the undocumented alien struggling to send money to sustain an impoverished family back home.

To Stay or to Go

Given that the majority of Brazilian immigrants are sojourners not settlers when they arrive in New York, the decision to stay in the United States is an about-face for most of them; it is a change of their original plan. What are the factors that go into such a major decision? Timing is one. As the length of stay in the United States increases, it becomes ever more difficult to return home since "it implies starting all over again in Brazil" (Martes

1995:9). Length of stay, in turn, often correlates with legal status, which also affects the decision to stay or to go. With some exceptions, the longer immigrants have lived in this country the more likely they are to have green cards and the greater the likelihood they will not go back to Brazil to live. And, having lived in the United States, immigrants have more information about what life is like in this country and what the option of returning to Brazil entails.

Gender also can be an important variable in the stay-or-go equation. One study of Brazilian immigrant women after their return home suggests why many are reluctant to do so (DeBiaggi 2004). A majority of returnees felt that their relationships with their husbands were better when they lived in the United States—that they were more independent and that there was more equality in the division of household tasks. Many resented their loss of autonomy and spoke wistfully of their years in the United States. I found similar sentiments in my own interviews in Brazil with returned migrant women who expressed dissatisfaction with "the way things were," that is, with traditional gender power relations, including the customary sexual division of labor. The most common refrain in these conversations was the "freedom and independence" that emigration had given them (Margolis 1997, 2001).

The findings on other immigrant groups are also suggestive. Some immigrant women in New York's Dominican community were reluctant to go home because they knew their nation's division of labor by gender and social class made their employment prospects dim. In order to delay the departure from New York, some Dominican women bought expensive durable goods like furniture and large household items. "This strategy serves both to root the family securely and comfortably in the U.S. and to deplete the funds needed to relocate," note the researchers who conducted the study (Grasmuck and Pessar 1992:156). Moreover, many of the immigrant women who did return to the Dominican Republic said they were dissatisfied with traditional gender roles there, missed paid employment, and resented their renewed economic dependence on their husbands.

Roughly half of the male and female immigrants in my own study said they planned to return to Brazil, but unlike the findings on female migrants mentioned above, fewer women than men said they definitely intended to stay in the United States. The likely reason for this disparity is that most of the immigrant women I studied were single, while research suggests that it is *married* women who are most reluctant to go home to resume their traditional domestic lifestyles.

The Matter of Children

Children may also play a role in the decision to stay in the United States, a decision that comes at a different time in the lives of immigrants than their initial decision to migrate. Immigrants are older and often have families; providing better opportunities for their children can be a powerful motive for remaining in this country. Children, especially teenagers, who have spent years in the United States may express their reluctance to go back to a country they hardly know. Moreover, American-born children help change immigrants' perspectives of the future. As Teresa Sales (2007) notes in her research on Brazilians in Boston, with an American citizen in the family an immigrant begins to feel more like an authentic, long-term participant in U.S. society.

But what of these children? At the time of my initial research in the early 1990s the question of children did not arise because, as we have seen, most Brazilians were young and many were single. Now with the passage of time a new generation of Brazilians has appeared, most of whom can be more precisely described as the "1.5 generation," that is, Brazilians who came to the United States as young children and are now adolescents (Portes 1990; Suárez-Orozco and Suárez-Orozco 2001).

What little research has been done on this generation is contradictory. One study of Brazilians in Massachusetts suggests that many of the 1.5 and second generation students have different expectations than their parents (Johnson 2004). Their parents—many of whom say they plan to return to Brazil someday—are willing to work in low-level jobs because they see them as temporary. But Brazilian adolescents often envision their residence in the United States as long-term or permanent and claim that they would be dissatisfied working in the same sort of low-wage service jobs held by their parents.

But other research, also in Massachusetts, suggests that many Brazilian adolescents do not reject the employment trajectory of their parents. Rather, many in this new generation reproduce the path of the parental generation in terms of jobs and values. This study found that most young Brazilians not only go to school fulltime, but that the vast majority also have extensive work experience. Moreover, they work in jobs similar to those of their parents: in supermarkets, restaurants, and construction, and as housecleaners and baby sitters. And it is work that most distinguishes their lives in the United States and Brazil. While in Brazil they led the carefree lives of children—playing and going to school; in the United States, because of their jobs, they are part of the adult world (Sales 2007).

Work, in turn, opens up the world of consumerism to these adolescents. About half used their earnings to help support their families; the rest worked not from necessity but to have their own money to do as they wished. Like the Brazilian immigrants I interviewed in New York City in the early 1990s, these young people cited the ability to earn so much more money in so much less time as the key motivation for living in the United States (Sales 2007).

Within this environment school is secondary, and parents who work long hours have little time to oversee their children's schooling. Education is viewed instrumentally, as a way of learning English in order to earn money, rather than as an end in itself. Relatively few see it as preparation for a move up the occupational ladder. As a result, the future of these young people in terms of their insertion in the U.S. labor market looks very much like that of their parents. While with experience they may eventually get somewhat better paying jobs, many are likely to remain confined to the unskilled service sector of the urban economy (Sales 2007).

The lack of mobility in the U.S. job market for many Brazilians has been confirmed by other research (Scudeler 1999). Then, too, evidence suggests that without higher education Brazilians are likely to be mired in the low-wage sector of the U.S. economy. As a result of shifts in the American labor market that have led to a steep decline in high-paying, unionized factory jobs—jobs typically held by those with only a high school education—today a man with a college degree earns, on average, 80 percent more than a man with only a high school diploma (Egan 2005).

So clearly one key to mobility in the U.S. labor market is higher education. Yet despite the aspirations of some Brazilian youth, the undocumented status of many is a serious handicap. One of the biggest challenges facing Brazilian adolescents is that—though having lived in this country for many years but because of their irregular status—in many states, including Massachusetts, they must pay out-of-state tuition if they want to attend a community college or state university, tuition that can cost two or three times that paid by legal residents (Souza 2004). One recent example of the consequences of this obstacle involves an undocumented Brazilian who was valedictorian of his high school class in Massachusetts but was unable to enroll in a public university because his parents could not afford out-of-state tuition and he was ineligible for other financial aid. Although he was a brilliant student with a bright future in computer science, his family returned to Brazil so that he could enroll in a tuition-free federal university there (Woolhouse 2005; de Oliveira 2005).

As a result of these barriers and the great personal frustration that often results, an indeterminate number of young Brazilians have become high school dropouts. In fact, Brazilian adolescents in Massachusetts have among the highest dropout rates of any immigrant community in the state. As a consequence, this limited access to higher education likely will effect future earnings (Andreazzi 2004; Johnson 2004).

The Return Home

What about the other side of the stay-or-go equation? Why do immigrants return to Brazil, some even after several years in the United States? Here, too, the reasons are many. Some immigrants simply get fed up with the grinding hours of work and the illusive goal of saving enough money for some ill-defined purpose back home. This is particularly true of older immigrants who came to the United States because a son or daughter had preceded them to this country (Martes 1995). Others return to Brazil precisely because they *have* met their objective and have enough savings to buy an apartment or start a small business. These are the "target earners" mentioned earlier, immigrants who came to the United States with the sole intention of saving money to meet some specific goal in Brazil. Still others never really adjust to life in the United States or may be unwilling to continue living so far from family and friends.

Once again, legal status can be a factor. As we have seen, obtaining a green card anchors some immigrants to the United States, but for others the opposite is true. Although it seems paradoxical, receiving a green card can figure prominently in the decision to return to Brazil. One would think that having a green card and being able to work legally would be a strong incentive to stay in the United States, but possessing this document actually provides still another option. Immigrants with green cards who return to Brazil and come to regret their decision can simply remigrate to the United States within a year, usually with no problem. Ironically, having a green card may make it easier to return home.

Because of the ease of travel, many of those with green cards or U.S. citizenship frequently visit Brazil.[2] Moreover, even Brazilians who are well established in the United States— those who are legal, own a house, have a good job, or own a business—say that they intend to return to Brazil "someday"—but only when they retire or their children are grown. As such, "the dream of returning is always present" (Siqueira 2005:19).

Of course, many immigrants are in a quandary about the decision to stay or to go. In my own study, some 20 percent were undecided about the future. In these cases, there is often a condition attached to the return home: I will go back to Brazil if the economy there improves, if inflation remains low, if I ever save enough money to buy an apartment, if good jobs open up for engineers, architects, teachers. . . . Or conversely, I'll stay in New York if I get a green card, if I get a job here I like, if I marry my American girlfriend (or boyfriend). A conditional return is often a delayed return and the reasons for the delay can be situated in the United States or in Brazil. For example, as a result of New York's economic recession of the early 1990s, some immigrants said that they kept delaying the return home because it had taken them longer to reach their goal of saving a particular sum of money. At the same time, others went back to Brazil when recession-induced unemployment reached 10 percent in New York, robbing them of their jobs in the city. In the mid-1990s, with inflation in Brazil under control for the first time in decades, Brazilians were more upbeat about the future of their country and this presumably spurred the return home of many.

After the beginning of the new millennium several additional factors came into play in the decision to stay or to go, particularly for Brazilians without work papers. The inability to get or renew drivers' licenses in many states, the 50 percent decline of the value of the dollar vis-à-vis the Brazilian currency during the early years of the new millenium, the fall-off in construction jobs due to the U.S. housing crisis, and the failure in 2007 of the U.S. Congress to pass immigration reform legislation that might have provided a path to legalization were all catalysts for the decision of a number of Brazilians to return home (Bernstein and Dwoskin 2007; Margolis 2008).

How do all of these individual decisions translate into real numbers? How many Brazilians actually return home to stay? How many remain in the United States? And how many go back to Brazil "for good" only to turn around and try to come back to this country? While real numbers are illusive, I was able to relocate a little more than two-thirds of the one hundred Brazilian immigrants in my study eighteen months after first interviewing them. Of these, 70 percent were still living in New York, 5 percent were residing elsewhere in the United States, and 25 percent had returned to Brazil. In other words, about 75 percent of the immigrants I was able to locate were still residing in this country a year and a half after the original interview. It is possible that many, if not most, of those I could not find had returned to Brazil and it is also possible that in the years following still more immigrants went back to Brazil to live. Finally, some of those now in the United States said they had actually returned to Brazil "for good" since the time of the interview, but had then remigrated to this country.

Going Home for Good?

Immigration in the jet age is often more circular than linear, a genuinely transnational process with waves of migrants moving back and forth across international borders, at times covering great distances. These movements may involve what I call yo-yo migration, the remigration of immigrants who have purportedly returned home "for good" (Margolis 1994:263). One study of Brazilian immigrants in the New York metropolitan area found that, either for economic reasons or because they could not adapt to life back home, half of those who returned to Brazil and had planned to stay then turned around and traveled back to the United States (Siqueira 2005).[3]

Despite the distance involved, I met several Brazilians in New York who had been traveling back and forth between Brazil and the United States for more than a decade. In other words, yo-yo migration may involve more than one "permanent" trip home. For example, over the ten years Paulo had lived in New York City he returned to Brazil three times "for good." Twice he stayed for more than a year before remigrating to the United States, the last time marrying and returning with his wife. They now have an American-born child. Said one of his friends, "Everyday Paulo's going to Brazil to live and six months later—here he comes again!" When I interviewed him Paulo insisted he was returning home "to try again." The last I heard he had gone back to Brazil "permanently," but his friend told me that Paulo plans to visit the United States once a year to maintain his status as a legal immigrant with a green card. After all, he never knows when it might come in handy!

Given the cost and distances involved, yo-yo migration between the United States and Brazil is more frequent than one would expect. Several times I was told of Brazilians who had gone back to Brazil for good, two, three, even four times, only to remigrate to the United States. In the words of the political scientist Wayne Cornelius, these yo-yo migrants come closer to "commuting" than to "immigrating" (quoted in Grant 1981:14). Such returnees have been called "shuttle migrants" and "cultural commuters," people who move back and forth between home and host country and are never quite satisfied with their lives in either one. Studies suggest that some of these migrants are disillusioned when they return home and that homesickness in the host country is replaced by discontent with conditions in the homeland, a kind of reverse culture shock (Gmelch 1980; Bernard and Ashton-Vouyoucalos 1976; Bernard and Comitas 1978).

What explains this pattern of indecision, this bouncing back and forth between Brazil and the United States? Why did some immigrants who talked of little else but going home to Brazil return there only to start planning their trips back to New York? In the early 1990s hyperinflation was the major catalyst for yo-yo migration. After returning home Brazilian immigrants soon found that the money saved in the United States provided little financial cushion in an economy with an inflation rate of 20 to 40 percent a month. But even after inflation was brought under control in 1994, the price of consumer goods in Brazil remained very high, particularly compared to the cost of similar items in the United States. People in the middle strata of Brazilian society had difficulty making ends meet as the cost of certain items—rent, medical care, school tuition, and other services—soared above the overall rate of inflation with no general increase in salaries. This, in turn, led to sky-high credit card debt and a rash of personal bankruptcies (Peluso and Goldberg 1995; O Globo 1995).

Economic conditions in Brazil did improve during the first years of the new millenium. Inflation remained low, credit became easier to get and less costly, and domestic consumption increased (Downie 2008). Still, the stability in the Brazilian economy did not lead to a mass return home. According to the director of the Center for Brazilian Immigrants in Massachusetts, "for now, the good news about the growth of the economy in Brazil hardly feeds the hope that, when they return, the situation in the country will be better (quoted in Pereira 2008).

Moreover, returned migrants did not easily forget their relatively generous New York wages. As one Brazilian said of her compatriots, "They're working full-time in Brazil and maybe earning $400 a month and they just can't forget that they were earning $400 a week in New York. They are always thinking about that, about how much more they used to earn there. It really bothers them and that's what spurs them to return to the United States."

The following scenario was played out time and again. Returned migrants used their savings to buy an apartment in Brazil but then could not find a suitable job or, if they did get a job, soon learned how difficult it was to make ends meet on Brazilian wages. While they now had a nice place to live, that was not enough to anchor them permanently to their homeland. The lack of jobs that paid reasonably well was a major irritant that spurred remigration. Returnees with high levels of education and skill were likely to face the same economic barriers in Brazil—the dearth of decent paying jobs that made use of their talents—that had led them to migrate in the first place.

Still, going home to Brazil, regretting the decision, and then returning to the United States is not as easy as one might think, and after September 11, 2001, it became much more difficult. For immigrants without green cards remigration can be a serious problem. I heard many tales of Brazilian immigrants who returned to Brazil with the intention of remaining there, changed their minds, and then found it difficult or impossible to get tourist visas to get back into this country. Recall that would-be "tourists" suspected of being immigrants are routinely denied visas by American consular personnel. When this happened to one yo-yo migrant he was so anxious to return to New York that he paid $4,000 for the documents—fake income tax returns and business ownership papers—needed to obtain a tourist visa.

Similar difficulties often befall undocumented Brazilians who live in the United States and want to go back to Brazil to see relatives and friends or take care of business there. The following episode, while extreme, highlights the problem. João, an undocumented immigrant who had lived in New York for several years and owned a small flooring company in Queens, flew to Brazil when he received word that his elderly father was terminally ill. João's Brazilian wife, Gisele, and their American-born daughter, Nara, remained behind in New York. When João returned to the United States he was stopped at Kennedy Airport by American immigration officers, questioned, and deported to Brazil because of evidence that he had previously overstayed his tourist visa. Gisele had no desire to return to Brazil to live and João, stuck in his hometown of Belo Horizonte, was so desperate to get back to his family and his business in the United States that he eventually did so by spending thousands of dollars to buy a passport with the coveted tourist visa stamped in it, both documents bearing someone else's name.

Are They Still Coming?

Are Brazilian immigrants still arriving in New York and other American cities in search of jobs, or has the improved economy back home slowed down or even halted the desire to seek one's fortune abroad? What impact did New York's economic downturn have on this migration stream? And what is the perspective of Brazilian immigrants already in the United States on these issues? Have economic conditions in New York and Brazil influenced their decisions to stay in this country or return home? The conditions confronting Brazilians and other immigrants after September 11, 2001, are discussed in the postscript.

While I completed my formal research prior to the implementation of the Brazilian economic plan that sharply curbed inflation, both my own anecdotal evidence and the findings of other researchers suggest that the improved economy neither stemmed the immigration flow nor caused Brazilians to return home en masse. Although precise figures do not exist, immigrants in Brazilian communities in New York, Boston, and south Florida report that their compatriots are still arriving from Brazil. The researcher Cristina Martes, who interviewed Brazilians in Boston who came to the United States *after* the new economic plan went into effect, suggests that because would-be immigrants make travel plans months or years in advance, new arrivals had been planning to immigrate to this country well before inflation was brought under control in Brazil. Moreover, their lives had not been sufficiently affected by changes in the Brazilian economy to make them reconsider their long-term goal of seeking work in the United States (Martes 2000).

Still, some observers of the immigrant scene insist that by the late 1990s fewer Brazilians were immigrating to this country. Greater optimism about the Brazilian economy was only one factor in the slowdown, they say, and perhaps a minor one at that. The much greater difficulty that Brazilians have had getting U.S. tourist visas was at least as important in dampening the transnational flow as any improvement in the Brazilian economy.

Since the primary attraction of the United States for immigrants is jobs, it is the health of urban labor markets in this country probably more than anything else that affects the level of immigration and return. Evidence suggests that from the 1990s onward, Brazilians and other immigrants encountered fewer job opportunities in New York, Boston, and other cities and, as a result, some newly arrived Brazilian immigrants who could not find work promptly turned around and went home.

Has New York's economic squeeze meant that fewer immigrants are arriving from Brazil in the first place? While there is no question that Brazilian immigrants are still coming to the city, a weaker job market probably has reduced the number somewhat. But, immigrants themselves disagreed on this point. While many in New York's Brazilian community were convinced that the city's economic downturn and subsequent rise in unemployment had caused a significant decline in Brazilian immigration, others argued that the flow of new arrivals from Brazil had not abated very much, if at all. "They're still coming, they're still coming," said a Baptist minister who serves New York's Brazilian community. Similarly, a Brazilian priest who ministers to a congregation of co-ethnics in the New York metropolitan area points out that in 2000 an average of some 450 people showed up for mass on Saturday and Sunday but by 2004 the number had grown to an average of about 750 (Maisonnave 2005b).

What about migration in the other direction? Has New York's economic slowdown influenced the decision of immigrants to return to Brazil? While many Brazilians did indeed leave the United States during the course of my research, their numbers and motivations were unclear. Nevertheless, nearly everyone I talked with agreed that it had become harder for immigrants to find work, and most thought that this was a major reason for the return home. The irony that some immigrants who went back to Brazil had been granted that much-coveted document—a green card—allowing them to work legally in the United States was not lost on their compatriots who remained behind in New York. "What good are documents if you can't find a job?" one asked. "After all, if you can't get work in either place, isn't it better to live in your own country?"

Here to Stay

Many Brazilian immigrants have lived in New York since the initial immigration surge from their country in the late 1980s. But at what point do these sojourners become settlers, people who see their future and the future of their children in their adopted land? How do Brazilians go from a mind-set utterly focused on the return home to one that imagines a future in the United States? Changes in attitude and behavior are part of the passage from temporary resident to permanent settler. Subtle signs provide clues to this gradual shift, and both work life and home life are affected by it. As more and more immigrants go through this process of transition, a community of sojourners is transformed into a community of settlers (Piore 1979).

Over time immigrants become less willing to spend long days laboring away at jobs that go nowhere. They grow more reluctant to work extra hours or to hold down a second job. Working shorter hours, they earn less money, but they spend more of it on leisure. They eat out at restaurants and go to the movies more often or they are more likely to buy tickets to a concert or a sporting event. They may start to take trips outside the city, to Washington, D.C., to see the nation's capitol or to Florida to visit Disney World. Some even begin buying more warm clothes, deciding that a new winter coat is really not an extravagance if they are going to spend another year or two in New York City's frosty clime.

Less time at work means more time is spent at home. Small cramped apartments with multiple roommates begin to grate on everyone's nerves. Brazilian immigrants start to think that having fewer people share an apartment might be worth the extra cost, while immigrant couples who rent out rooms may eventually decide that the additional money is just not worth the loss of privacy. As their stay in New York lengthens, many Brazilians become dissatisfied with their spartan home life and they begin spending money to fix up their apartments. While even the sparsely furnished dwellings of recent immigrants are often packed with computers, stereo equipment, televisions, DVDs, and state-of-the-art answering machines, it is understood that this electronic gear was actually purchased for the return home. But when immigrants begin renovating their apartments or buying major pieces of furniture or large appliances that cannot be easily transported back to Brazil, it becomes evident that they no longer see their New York lives as "here today and gone tomorrow."

The process continues. Time passes, living conditions in New York slowly improve, and the return home is put off for yet another year. Since immigrants are spending more on their lives in New York and saving less for the return to Brazil, their initial plan of going home with a certain sum of money in hand remains a distant goal. But, appearances to the contrary, many Brazilian immigrants *still* insist that they are planning to return home. Studies suggest that even after a number of their own deadlines for departure have passed, immigrants often cling to what has become a myth of return. Some, in fact, hold to an ideology of return no matter *how* long they have been in their adopted country (Castro 1985; Papademetriou and DiMarzio 1986; Gmelch 1980). Perhaps this is why every immigrant interviewed for a magazine article about the Brazilian diaspora spoke of the immigrants' ultimate goal: "When I'm old I want to return to Brazil and be buried there."

Postscript

Brazilian Immigrants and September 11, 2001

On November 14, 2001, the Brazilian consulate in New York City ran a prominent ad in the *New York Times* requesting that anyone having information on the whereabouts of the thirteen Brazilian citizens listed in the ad contact the consulate. Unstated was the fact that all had been missing since September 11 and were presumed to have been killed in the terrorist attack on the World Trade Center. I have no doubt that several of the Brazilians named in the ad were immigrants who were working as shoeshiners or busboys or in other low-paying jobs in the twin towers. Indeed, during my earlier research I interviewed many Brazilians who were employed as shoeshiners in Manhattan office buildings, including the World Trade Center itself. But the precise number of Brazilians killed in the attack probably will never be known. So many who toiled there were undocumented immigrants who worked "off the books" and who left no paper trail of their employment.

But the impact of this event on Brazilian immigrants was not limited to the victims themselves and the families of those who lost their lives in the attack. It had both immediate and long-term consequences for Brazilians and other immigrants in the city and across the country. According to an article in the *New York Times*, "the terrorists may have aimed at capitalists, but they hit low-paying jobs hardest" (Eaton and Wyatt 2001). The sweeping round of layoffs following the attack and the subsequent decline in travel meant that thousands lost their jobs in the airline, hotel, and restaurant industries, all of which employ large numbers of immigrant workers. In the weeks after September 11, for example, officials of the Hotel and Restaurant Employees International Union reported that in nine major American cities between 25 and 40 percent of the union's heavily immigrant work force had been laid off. In fact, more restaurant workers and cleaners lost their jobs as a result of the attacks and the ensuing economic decline and rise in unemployment than any other job category (Dillon 2001; Eaton and Wyatt 2001).

What about the lure of the United States for current and would-be immigrants right after the attacks in New York and Washington? For many Brazilians it was buried under the rubble of the World Trade Center that fateful September morning. Contemporary press reports in Brazil suggested that many would-be immigrants were reconsidering their plans, while others already living in the United States were thinking about returning home. "I'm terrified," one Brazilian in New York City was quoted as saying. "Besides fearing new attacks, I feel that all immigrants now are going to be discriminated against" (quoted in Dalevi 2001). The publisher of *Brazilian Times*, a Portuguese-language newspaper in Boston, noted that right after the attacks a number of Brazilians began selling their cars and furniture in preparation for the return to Brazil. "My paper is filled with ads from Brazilians selling what they can. Besides fear, there is this sensation that there will be a wave of xenophobia against immigrants. It is going to be very hard to get a job from now on," he said (quoted in Dalevi 2001).

Evidence suggests that while there was no mass exodus of Brazilians from the United States after the terrorist attacks, "Eldorado has less shine," to quote the title of an article on the impact of September 11 in *Veja*, Brazil's most widely read newsmagazine. Soon after the attacks, a Brazilian priest in Astoria, Queens, a major Brazilian residential enclave, said that he was seeing fewer new parishioners arriving from Brazil. "At Sunday mass when we introduce newcomers to the congregation, we used to have an average [of] ten every Sunday. Today, there are rarely more than four" (quoted in Salgado 2002). At least for a time, then, the United States had become a less-attractive place for Brazilian immigrants.

But what of the long-term impact of the events of September 11 on Brazilians and other immigrants in the United States? How have the events changed their lives? One serious problem for immigrants that has arisen since the attacks is what was once the relatively simple act of obtaining a driver's license. Prior to that terrible day many states did not require applicants to have a Social Security card before a driver's license could be issued. But since then most states have made it far more difficult to get or even renew licenses without proper documentation. Because a driver's license is not only required to operate a vehicle and take out car insurance but also is often needed to open a bank account, get a credit card, enter a federal building, rent an apartment, or travel, the lack of a license presents ongoing problems in daily life. Said one Brazilian about the current situation, "It is better to be deported than to live here without a driver's license. Without it we become invisible. Having [a license] . . . is the closest you can get to being American. Only the green card is better."[1]

Since September 11, issuing driver's licenses to undocumented immigrants has also emerged as an incendiary political issue. While immigrant advocacy groups have been lobbying to allow undocumented immigrants to obtain driver's licenses, arguing that this insures that they will have passed a driver's test, know the rules of the road, and can get car insurance, anti-immigrant groups have been just as vehement in opposing the awarding of such documents to "illegal aliens." Most alarming to immigrant advocates is the Real ID Act passed by the U.S. Congress in May 2005. Once fully implemented, the legislation mandates that applicants for driver's licenses in *all fifty states* must prove they are in the United States legally.

Then, too, some local officials have taken it upon themselves to challenge the residence in their communities of Brazilians and other immigrants who lack driver's licenses or documents proving that they are living in the United States legally. For example, although immigration control is a federal responsibility, in Danbury, Connecticut, which has a sizeable Brazilian population, the mayor sought to deputize the state police to enforce immigration laws. Similarly, the police chief in a small town in New Hampshire has invented his own border control policy; he has given orders to arrest undocumented immigrants, charging that they are "trespassing" in his community (O'Leary 2005; Powell 2005). To be sure, these and similar moves have been challenged in court. Immigrant advocates were cheered by a judicial decision in 2007 that declared the enforcement of immigration laws to be strictly a federal responsibility, rather than a state or local one, but they were disheartened by other judicial findings that backed local efforts to crack down on illegal immigration (Preston 2007, 2008b).

But the repercussions of September 11, 2001, have been much broader than its impact on driver's licenses and the actions of a few scattered officials. Entering the United States also has become much more problematic for foreigners, especially would-be immigrants. After September 11 obtaining a tourist visa became even more difficult than it was during the 1990s. One result of the growing obstacles placed in the path of Brazilians seeking U.S. tourist visas was a huge increase in the number of Brazilians entering the United States through Mexico. Brazilians flew to Mexico City, made their way to the U.S. border by bus or car, then with the help of smugglers crossed into the United States at border points in Texas and Arizona—sometimes after walking across miles of desert.

Although no hard figures exist, it appears that a majority of Brazilian immigrants arriving in the United States in the years immediately following September 11 were entering via Mexico. One study of Brazilians who arrived in the United States *after* 2000 found that three-quarters entered illegally either via Mexico or by using a false passport upon arrival at U.S. immigration (Maisonnave 2005a, 2005d; Siqueira 2005). Moreover, the stories of border crossings from Mexico are legion. Here's one: "I went through Mexico and it took fifteen days. I spent two days and two nights in the wild, without eating or drinking. We were a group of nineteen Brazilians." And another: "My brother almost died in the river. There were eighteen Brazilians in their underwear crossing the river . . . one person would carry a plastic bag with all the clothes" (quoted in Marcus 2008).

An inquiry in 2005 by the Brazilian Congress into undocumented immigration to the United States uncovered nearly forty smuggling rings that brought immigrants from Brazil to the United States through Mexico. *Consul* is the slang term for human smuggler used in the small Brazilian cities and towns where smugglers recruit would-be immigrants who seek to enter the United States via Mexico (Marcus 2008). This "smuggling mafia" was found to be well organized and highly profitable. According to the inquiry, these organizations made loans to prospective immigrants who wanted to travel to the United States but who lacked the smuggler's fee of $10,000 and up. Houses, cars, or other properties in Brazil were used as collateral with the understanding that the loan—plus up to 10 percent monthly interest— would be repaid once the immigrant arrived in the United States and found work (Comissão Parlamentar Mista de Inquérito da Emigração 2006; Mineo 2005).

As a consequence, after September 11 the number of Brazilians who entered the United States via Mexico skyrocketed. A few figures bear this out. By 2005 Brazilians were the fastest growing group of "other than Mexicans," or OTMs in the parlance of U.S. immigration, detained at the border. Some 31,000 Brazilians were stopped during the first ten months of 2005, an increase of almost 900 percent over three years. As such, Brazil had become among the top four nations of origin for illegal entries via Mexico, behind only Honduras and El Salvador and, of course, Mexico (Donohue 2005; Maisonnave 2005c, 2005d).

One key to this influx is that Brazilians—and other immigrants as well— were taking advantage of a loophole in U.S. immigration policy. According to international law, when "other than Mexicans" are stopped at the border, they cannot be sent back to Mexico; they must be returned to their own countries. Since the United States has long had a severe shortage of detention space, very few of those apprehended were imprisoned before being sent home. Instead, they were given a summons ordering them to appear in court at some future date. Upwards of 98 percent of those so detained, however, never showed up. Once Brazilians learned of this procedure, that is, that if they were stopped they would be let go after being given a court summons and could then travel to their final destination in the United States, many purposely allowed themselves to be caught by the Border Patrol (Kammer 2005). Consequently, the increase in the number of Brazilians detained may, in part, be an artifact of a change in their behavior based on new knowledge of border procedures.

Toward the end of 2005, however, this situation changed dramatically. At the behest of the U.S. government, Mexico reimposed a visa requirement for Brazilians entering that country. Then as vehement demands to "control the border" grew louder in the United States, a new policy was instituted that required the immediate arrest and deportation of all OTMs caught on the border. These two factors appear to have stemmed the influx of undocumented Brazilians into the United States via the frontier with Mexico.

Evidence that these measures were having the intended effect comes from different sources. As noted above, the U.S. Border Patrol reported that during 2005 over 31,000 Brazilians were detained on the U.S.-Mexico border for an average of 85 people per day. But during the first three months of 2006, once the "rapid removal" program and Mexican visa requirement were in place, only 215 Brazilians were detained for an average of about 2.3 per day, the lowest rate since 2001 (Maisonnave 2006a; 2006b). Then, too, the director of the Brazilian Immigrant Center in Massachusetts noted in April 2006 that since December 2005 he had not encountered "a single Brazilian who had entered the U.S. via Mexico" (quoted in Sotero 2006).

The new OTM deportation program was loudly trumpeted as a success by Michael Chertoff (2006), the U.S. Director of Homeland Security, and by President George W. Bush, both of whom specifically cited the decline in undocumented Brazilians picked up on the border: "We're . . . pursuing . . . common sense steps to accelerate the deportation process. . . . We recently tested the effectiveness of these steps with Brazilian illegal immigrants caught along the Rio Grande Valley of the Texas border. The effort was called Operation Texas Hold 'Em. It delivered impressive results. Thanks to our actions, Brazilian illegal immigration dropped by 90 percent in the Rio Grande Valley, and by 50 to 60 percent across the border as a whole" (Bush 2005).

With the requirement that Brazilians get visas to travel to Mexico, a new and more dangerous route to the United States via Guatemala was established. Some days before the new Mexican visa requirement went into effect at least sixty Brazilians were detained in Mexico near the frontier with Guatemala, which does not require Brazilians to have tourist visas. The sixty detainees were from a number of regions in Brazil, suggesting that the scheme to employ this new route was widespread in that country (McKinley 2007; Maisonnave and Guimarães 2005; Reel 2006).

September 11 and Transnationalism

There was yet another change in behavior on the part of Brazilians and other immigrants in the United States after the attacks in 2001. This is the impact of September 11 on transnationalism. One of the most salient features of transnational migration is the movement of international migrants back and forth between home and host countries. While the frequency of such international travel varies with geographical distance and financial resources, one of the basic ingredients of transnationalism is that international migrants do not leave their home countries never to return (Glick Schiller, Basch, and Blanc-Szanton 1992).

Since September 11, 2001, however, it has become much more difficult for Brazilian immigrants as well as other immigrants—unless they have green cards—to be transnationals, to be territorially mobile, that is, to travel easily back and forth between the United States and their own countries.[2] While what I previously called "yo-yo migration," the remigration of Brazilians to the United States who had purportedly returned home for good, was still possible prior to September 11, with growing strictures on the issuance of tourist visas and greater control at airports, such travel has become ever more problematic (Margolis 1994, 2008).

Seasonal workers, that is, those with jobs in construction and landscaping who typically are employed only part of the year, illustrate the predicament of some Brazilian immigrants. Where they once returned to Brazil during the slow winter months when work was scarce, today they cannot risk such travel and are forced to remain in the United States even if unemployed. Similar difficulties often befall undocumented Brazilians who live in the United States and want to go back to Brazil just to visit relatives and friends or take care of business there.

New obstacles to transnational migration among Brazilians are evident in the remarks of one immigrant in New York City in 2006: "When illegal

Brazilians decide to go back to Brazil, this decision means that they must accept [the fact] that they will never live in New York again. Therefore, they need to consider, before leaving, whether they want to stay temporarily or otherwise in New York" (quoted in Strategier 2006:42). Similarly, two researchers referring to Brazilians in Boston note that "this back-and-forth movement [to Brazil] now is far from being frequent, if not impossible, for many . . . immigrants" (De Lourenço and McDonnell 2004). And the advice of one attorney with a large Brazilian clientele in Danbury, Connecticut, is likely now common among those who counsel undocumented immigrants throughout the United States: "Stay here or go home," he said. "Don't go back and forth" (Boyle 2004).

Further evidence of the strictures on international travel comes from the former liaison to the immigrant community at the Brazilian consulate in New York City. She told me that she received daily calls from frantic Brazilians at Kennedy Airport who have been barred from entering or reentering the United States. In nearly all cases, they are denied entry even if they have valid visas and passports because they had overstayed the time limit of their visas on a previous occasion, which meant that they had been living in the United States illegally and, therefore, were prohibited from returning. Air manifests are now screened in advance and passengers may be sent back to Brazil upon arrival in the United States if there is evidence that they were undocumented in the past. One Brazilian airline that had had on average two passengers a month barred from entering the United States by immigration agents prior to September 11 has had *at least one passenger a day* turned away since the attacks (Boyle 2004; Salgado 2002).

To be sure, Brazilians are not the only immigrants experiencing such problems. Data from Mexico also indicate a brake on transnationalism. Evidence suggests that even prior to September 11, 2001, the number of border crossers had declined as border controls were tightened and the costs of returning home increased. But, as researchers referring to Mexican immigration to the United States have noted, "a perverse consequence of draconian border enforcement is that it does not deter would-be migrants from trying to enter the country so much as *it discourages those who are already here from returning home*" (Massey, Durand, and Malone 2002:128–29, emphasis added). In other words, as the difficulty of reentering the United States escalates for immigrants either through border buildups or visa denials, their stay in this country is prolonged, return migration becomes less likely, and a shift toward permanent settlement occurs.

These constraints seem to have changed the nature of Brazilian immigration. As we have seen, the majority of Brazilian immigrants to the United States, past and present, have always claimed they would eventually go back to Brazil after they had saved a requisite amount of money even though many delayed the return home for years or even decades. But today many recent immigrants, realizing that once they return to Brazil they must stay, have been meeting their monetary goals in three or four years and then actually going home for good.

A very different situation, however, is faced by Brazilians who have lived in the United States for five or ten or more years and who remain undocumented. Simply put, they are caught in a vise. Since it has become so difficult to come and go from the United States, they are loath to risk returning to Brazil only to find they cannot get a job or otherwise support themselves there. Even immigrants who have lost jobs in the United States are reluctant to return to Brazil without the savings they had planned, knowing they are also likely to be jobless back home. This feeling of entrapment has caused profound depression in some Brazilians, a feeling that they have "lost their place," that they cannot return to Brazil because if they return they cannot survive and if they stay in the United States they cannot live.

A Sea of Global Voyagers

Despite the obstacles erected after September 11, 2001, many Brazilian immigrants will still become true transnationals. They will continue to live in the United States and they will see their lives and future as intimately tied to the fortunes and future of their new country. But they will not forsake Brazil. They will still want to go home on visits, they will maintain regular contact with family members who remain there, and they will never stop thinking of themselves as Brazilians. Moreover, many are likely to retire to their native land.

The Brazilian transnational experience is just one variant of a global pattern. It is part of a world-wide phenomenon in which migrants from less industrialized nations travel what are often great distances to find work in the industrialized countries of North America, Europe, and Asia. Scholars of international migration have long sought to understand these global movements, some suggesting that the stream of peoples from newly industrializing states to industrialized states is, in part, fostered by a desire for improved consumption and an enhanced style of life (Portes and Bach 1985). These aspirations are tied to increased levels of education in migrant-exporting nations along with greater media exposure to consumer patterns in advanced industrial states. This helps explain why international migrants, like those from Brazil, often do not come from the poorest nations or from the most impoverished regions of their own nations.

International migration also can help diffuse worrisome social and economic problems within migrant-sending states. For example, in many Latin American and other newly industrializing economies, capital-intensive industrial and agricultural development has created labor surpluses. Labor surpluses stimulate emigration because they increase unemployment and depress wages and living standards, including, in some cases, living standards of the middle class. This is one reason why in recent years middle-class migrants from the industrializing world—like those from Brazil—have become part of these global movements.

The departure of well-educated migrants, in turn, helps alleviate the dilemma of the "overqualified" in many migrant-sending nations. As in the case of Brazil, the dilemma arises when large numbers of professionals are trained, but even though their skills are needed at home, not enough jobs are available at wages they deem adequate given their many years of schooling. Labor market realities in some developing nations, then, have stymied expectations of social mobility for a segment of their well-educated and highly trained citizenry. International migration diffuses the situation, in part, by sending many of the overqualified abroad.

The global travel of this educated "surplus" as well as of international migrants, in general, serves yet another important function. Given the low wages and underemployment that plague many industrializing nations, the remittance money that migrants send from their jobs abroad helps subsidize family members back home. By cushioning their families economically, migrants' remittances dissipate the political unrest that might arise among a disgruntled populace beset by low wages, falling living standards, and limited economic opportunities.

A few figures indicate just how important remittances are to the economies of some industrializing nations. Mexicans living in the United States, for example, sent over $15 billion in remittances home in 2004, while fully one-third of the income of the Dominican Republic comes from the dollars sent back by immigrants. Even in Brazil the estimated 2 million Brazilians living abroad—about 1 percent of the Brazilian population—are thought to have remitted the impressive sum of over $6 billion in 2005, about the same amount as the country earned from soybeans, its leading export (Luna 2005; Fisher 1996; Rohter 2005).

The benefits of international migration, however, do not flow in only one direction. Despite the anti-immigrant sentiment that is so much a part of contemporary discourse in the industrialized world, the truth is that host nations also gain immeasurably from these global currents. After all, the industrial nations that are the objects of transnational migrants' desire are in the enviable position of having a huge supply of cheap labor clamoring to fill jobs most citizens of their own lands reject out of hand (Piore 1979; 1986). And, as we have seen, advanced industrial countries are now even attracting well-educated, highly motivated immigrants—like middle-class Brazilians—for what are very menial jobs. Through legislation and selective enforcement of immigration laws, moreover, these nations can both generate a useful supply of inexpensive, powerless labor and partially regulate its conditions of entry.

Global voyagers are beneficial to advanced industrialized nations not only for the relatively low cost of their labor, but for their transience as well. Initially, at least, most international migrants view their stay abroad as temporary, often lasting only enough time to save money for the return home. It is this built-in impermanence that melds so neatly with the type of work that most immigrants do. As we have seen, international migrants, like Brazilians, are overwhelmingly employed in jobs with low wages, little job security, few or no benefits, low prestige, and little or no opportunity for advancement. Because of their many undesirable features, finding native-born workers to fill these jobs is difficult or impossible. But international migrants who see themselves as here today and gone tomorrow are more sanguine about the lack of career prospects and other liabilities of such work.

The benefits of transnational migration to the industrialized world are substantial. It provides a mass of low-cost, often well-educated workers who are willing, even eager, to take a variety of jobs that otherwise might go un-filled. And, at the same time, international migration relieves some of the economic and political pressures that might otherwise threaten the stability of many newly industrializing nations.

Notes

Preface

1. Because it has become an incendiary epithet, I have generally avoided using the phrase "illegal alien" throughout this book and have used "undocumented immigrant" or "immigrant without work papers" instead.

2. Itinerant consulates regularly travel to smaller cities and towns that have significant Brazilian immigrant populations. While there, consular personnel service the needs of the local Brazilian community.

Chapter 1. A New Ingredient in the Melting Pot

1. Brazilians are not limited to Queens; about 30 percent live in Manhattan, with smaller concentrations in the city's other boroughs.

2. The *cruzeiro* was the Brazilian unit of currency until July 1994, when it was replaced by the *real*. One *real* was worth about U.S.$0.61 in mid-2008.

3. In January 2004 the Department of Homeland Security began implementing the U.S.-Visit Program, a long-planned tracking program that requires millions of foreign visitors to submit digital fingerscans and a digital photograph upon arrival in the United States. While U.S.-Visit was mandated by Congress to be a full-scale entry and exit tracking program, more than three years after its implementation it still did virtually nothing to track visitors exiting the country (Stana 2007).

Chapter 2. Brazilian Immigrants: A Portrait

1. About 80 percent were from cities in just two Brazilian states—Minas Gerais and Rio de Janeiro—and most of the remainder were from the urban areas of São Paulo, Paraná, and Espirito Santo, all in south central and southern Brazil, the most prosperous region of the nation. By 2000, however, Brazilian immigrants to the United States came from sixteen states and the federal district. As such, the source of immigrants has expanded to the extent that today emigration has become a national phenomenon in Brazil (Martes 2000).

2. The Brazilian elite is composed of executives who run the city's Brazilian banks, airlines, and corporations and their families.

Chapter 3. Working New York

1. The federal minimum wage was finally raised to $5.85 an hour in 2007, rising to $7.25 an hour in 2009, after it had stagnated at $5.15 an hour over the preceding decade. The minimum wage in New York State was raised to $7.15 an hour in 2007.

2. In fact, a number of Brazilians wound up not needing cold weather clothes. Having lived in the Northeast they subsequently moved to south Florida, which they say they prefer because of the weather (Suarez 2003).

3. The other major provision of IRCA was the Amnesty Program. This was intended to legalize long-term undocumented immigrants, defined as those who had resided continually in the United States since 1982.

4. E-Verify, a voluntary federal program, allows employers to electronically verify new employees' legal authorization to work in the United States. However, by 2008 only 52,000 employers of 5.7 million employers nationally, or less than 1 percent, were using the system (Archibold 2008).

5. In full-service restaurants, waiters take food orders, food handlers deliver food and drinks to the table, and busboys clear away dirty dishes. Full-service restaurants are distinguished from fast food restaurants by having table service and other amenities.

6. An exception to this are the many Brazilians in the small New Jersey towns of Riverside and Burlington, most of whom work as carpenters, having learned their skills on the job (Moroz 2005a).

Chapter 4. Immigrant Life in Gotham City

1. After the attacks on September 11, 2001, the U.S. Immigration and Naturalization Service was incorporated into the newly created Department of Homeland Security and is now called Immigration Control and Enforcement or ICE.

2. In recent years police in some Brazilian cities, notably Rio de Janeiro and São Paulo, have been charged with rampant corruption and have been accused of murdering street children for pay.

3. The Brazilian Rainbow Group, although initially formed to aid gay and lesbian immigrants, has reached out and offered advice and aid to the immigrant population at large, making it the only such organization serving Brazilian immigrants in New York City. In Massachusetts, the Brazilian Immigrant Center, founded in the mid-1990s, is an important source of aid to Brazilian immigrants, particularly in employment-related matters.

4. In June 1996, Rudolph Giuliani, then the mayor of New York City, signed legislation officially naming West 46th Street in Manhattan "Little Brazil Street."

5. This festival, first held in 1984, features booths selling Brazilian food and drink, handicrafts, tapes, t-shirts, and all manner of items with Brazilian logos. Brazilian music blares from loudspeakers and the festival invariably ends with hundreds of merrymakers dancing the *samba* in the street.

6. The Universal Church has received extended criticism in the Brazilian press as a cult-like organization whose main concern is its own financial success, primarily achieved through the monetary contributions of its converts (Alvarez, Italiano, and Riberio 2000; *Veja* 1995a).

7. Milton Nascimento is a well-known Brazilian singer who has given sold-out concerts in New York's Radio City Music Hall.

8. *Caipirinhas* are potent drinks made of Brazilian cane alcohol, sugar, and freshly

squeezed limes. *Feijoada* (literally, "big bean") is the Brazilian national dish. It consists of assorted meats simmered in black beans and served with rice, kale, orange slices, toasted manioc flour, and hot sauce.

Chapter 5. Ethnicity, Race, and Gender

1. Concurrent with the article about Brazilians in Queens, the *New York Times* also featured a video on its web site, "Brazil in Queens" in which I was interviewed.

2. "Latino," meaning a person from Latin America, is a more inclusive term than Hispanic. Although all Hispanics are Latinos, not all Latinos are Hispanic. In fact, in her research among Brazilians in Boston, Helen Marrow (2004) found that second-generation Brazilians were far more willing to identify themselves as Latinos than were their parents.

3. About 250,000 Japanese-Brazilians have immigrated to Japan since the mid-1980s (Linger 2001). They are there for the same reason other Brazilians have gone to the United States: to take jobs that pay far more than they could earn in Brazil.

4. Women make up 44 percent of the low-wage immigrant work force in the United States (Abraham 2005b).

Chapter 6. From Sojourner to Settler

1. *My Grandmother Has a Video Camera* by Tania Cypriano is an engaging documentary from 2007 about a Brazilian grandmother from São Paulo who documents the life of her immigrant family in San Francisco.

2. Brazilians have been able to hold dual citizenship since 1994.

3. Since September 11, 2001, most of these returns were via Mexico, a topic discussed in the postscript.

Postscript. Brazilian Immigrants and September 11, 2001

1. In one scheme, "tours" to states where it is easier to get a driver's license were organized, tours that could cost up to $3,000. In another, a Brazilian sold over 1,700 counterfeit Social Security cards for $2,000 to $2,500 each. His arrest enabled U.S. authorities to trace hundreds of illegally obtained driver's licenses issued to Brazilians, which were then canceled (Mineo 2003).

2. Prior to September 11 those with green cards could continue to travel to the United States unimpeded as long as they did not remain out of the country for more than one year. However, since that date even some immigrants with green cards, who had stayed abroad for a few months have been stopped arbitrarily upon entry into the United States and told that they had remained away too long and could not be readmitted.

References

Abraham, Yvonne. 2005a. "Local Brazilians Say They're Targeted Unfairly." *Boston Globe*, Metro/Region, April 11, p. 8.

———. 2005b. "Immigrant Labor Force Booming." *Boston Globe*, Metro/Region, June 19, p. 1.

Alvarez, Maria, Laura Italiano, and Luiz C. Riberio. 2000. "Holy-Roller Church Cashes In on Faithful." *New York Post*, July 23.

Alves, José Claudio Souza, and Lúcia Ribeiro. 2002. "Migracão, Religião e Transnacionalismo: O Caso dos Brasileiros no Sul da Flórida." *Religião e Sociedade* 22(2): 65–90.

Andreazzi, Luciana. 2004. "Brazilian Immigrants: The Ecological Matrix of Social Exchange, Resources and Vulnerabilities." Paper presented at the Conference on Brazilians in the U.S. entitled "Another Invisible Latino Diaspora," Aliança Brasileira nos Estados Unidos, Central Connecticut State University, New Britain, April 16.

Araujo, Ledice. 1995. "Serviços: Altas de Até 200% São Difíceis de Engolir." *O Globo*, July 1, p. 4.

Archibold, Randal C. 2008. "U.S. Program to Verify Worker Status Growing." *New York Times*, February 13, p. 15.

Badgley, Ruey T. 1994. "Brazucas in Beantown: The Dynamics of Brazilian Ethnicity in Boston." Senior honors thesis in anthropology, Connecticut College, New London.

Basch, Linda, Nina Glick Schiller, and Cristina Szanton Blanc. 1994. *Nations Unbound: Transnational Projects, Postcolonial Predicaments, and Deterritorialized Nation-States.* Langhorne, Pa.: Gordon and Breach.

Bean, Frank D., Barry Edmonston, and Jeffery S. Passel, eds. 1990. *Undocumented Migration to the United States: IRCA and the Experience of the 1980s.* Santa Monica: Rand Corporation; Washington, D.C.: Urban Institute.

Bellos, Alex. 2002. "Rio Blames It on the Simpsons." *The Guardian*, April 9.

Beraba, Marcelo. 2007. "Os Que Voltam Não Têm Trabalho Nem Dinheiro, Afirma Socióloga." *Folha de São Paulo*, December 9.

Berger, Joseph, and Fernanda Santos. 2005. "Trading Status for a Raise." *New York Times*, December 26, pp. B1, B7.

Bernard, H. Russell. 2005. *Research Methods in Anthropology: Qualitative and Quantitative Approaches.* 4th ed. Walnut Creek, Calif.: AltaMira Press.

Bernard, H. Russell, and Sandy Ashton-Vouyoucalos. 1976. "Return Migration to Greece." *Journal of the Steward Anthropological Society* 8(1): 31–52.

Bernard, H. Russell, and Lambros Comitas. 1978. "Greek Return Migration." *Current Anthropology* 19(3): 658–59.

Bernstein, Nina, and Elizabeth Dwoskin. 2007. "For Many Brazilians Here Illegally, the Promised Land Has Lost Its Promise." *New York Times*, December 4, p. 32.

Beserra, Bernadete. 2003. *Brazilian Immigrants in the United States: Cultural Imperialism and Social Class*. New York: LFB Scholarly Publishing.

Bonacich, Edna, and John Modell. 1980. *The Economic Basis of Ethnic Solidarity: Small Business in the Japanese-American Community*. Berkeley: University of California Press.

Boyle, Michael. 2004. "Immigration Law, Legal Resources Available." Paper presented at the Conference on Brazilians in the U.S. entitled "Another Invisible Latino Diaspora," Aliança Brasileira nos Estados Unidos, Central Connecticut State University, New Britain, April 16.

Brazilian Voice. 1995. "Empresários Brasileiros Temerosos com a Blitz da Imigração." April 28–May 4.

Brenner, Leslie. 1991. "The New New York." *New York Woman*, April, pp. 68–81.

Briggs, Vernon M., Jr., and Stephen Moore. 1994. *Still an Open Door? U.S. Immigration Policy and the American Economy*. Washington, D.C.: American University Press.

Brimelow, Peter. 1995. *Alien Nation: Common Sense about America's Immigration Disaster*. New York: Random House.

Brooke, James. 1993. "In Brazil Wild Ways to Counter Wild Inflation." *New York Times*, July 25, p. 11.

———. 1994a. "Economy Dampens Ardor of Brazilians." *New York Times*, January 5, p. C11.

———. 1994b. "Brazilians Get Serious on Inflation and Deficit." *New York Times*, March 3, p. D2.

Brown, Peter. 2005a. "Understanding Brazuca 'Fragmentation': A Qualitative Study of Brazilian Immigrants and Their Community in Boston, Massachusetts." Paper presented at the National Congress on Brazilian Immigration to the United States, David Rockefeller Center for Latin American Studies, Harvard University, Cambridge, Mass., March 18–19.

———. 2005b. "The Ambivalent Immigrants: Brazilians and the Conflict of Ethnic Identity." Senior honors thesis in sociology and Brazilian and Portuguese studies, Harvard University, Cambridge, Mass.

Buchanan, Susan H. 1979. "Haitian Women in New York City." *Migration Today* 7(4): 19–25, 39.

Bush, George W. 2005. "President Discusses Border Security and Immigration Reform in Arizona." Department of Homeland Security, Davis-Monthan Air Force Base, Tucson, Ariz. http://www.whitehouse.gov/news/releases/2005/11/20051128-7.html, accessed November 18, 2005.

Butcher, Kristin F., and David Card. 1991. "Immigration and Wages: Evidence from the 1980s." *Economic Impact of Immigration* 81(2): 292–96.

Castro, Mary Garcia. 1985. "Work Versus Life: Colombian Women in New York." In *Women and Change in Latin America*, ed. June Nash and Helen Safa, 231–59. South Hadley, Mass.: Bergin and Garvey.

Chavez, Leo R. 1988. "Settlers and Sojourners: The Case of Mexicans in the United States." *Human Organization* 47(2): 95–107.

——. 1989. "Households, Migration, and Settlement: A Comparison of Undocumented Mexicans and Central Americans in the United States." Paper presented at the 88th annual meeting of the American Anthropological Association, Washington, D.C.

Cheever, Susan. 1995. "The Nanny Track." *The New Yorker*, March 6, pp. 84–95.

Chertoff, Michael. 2006. Remarks by Secretary of Homeland Security Michael Chertoff to the American Enterprise Institute, Washington, D.C. http://www.dhs.gov/xnews/speeches/speech_0285.shtm, accessed June 29, 2006.

Chigusa, Charles Tetsuo, ed. 1994. *A Quebra dos Mitos: O Fenômeno Dekassegui Através de Relatos Pessoais.* Mizuhiki, Japan: IPC Produção and Consultoria.

Colen, Shellee. 1990. "'Housekeeping' for the Green Card: West Indian Household Workers, the State, and Stratified Reproduction in New York." In *At Work in Homes: Household Workers in World Perspective,* ed. Roger Sanjek and Shellee Colen, 89–118. AES Monograph Series 3. Washington, D.C.: American Ethnological Society.

Comissão Parlamentar Mista de Inquérito da Emigração. 2006. "Relatório Final." Congresso Nacional, República Federativa do Brasil, Brasília.

Congressional Budget Office. 2006. "Historical Effective Tax Rates: 1979 to 2004." December, Table 1C.

Cornelius, Wayne A. 1982. "Interviewing Undocumented Immigrants: Methodological Reflections Based on Fieldwork in Mexico and the U.S." *International Migration Review* 16(2): 378–411.

Corrêa, Marcos Sá. 1994. "O Brasil Se Expande." *Veja,* September 7, pp. 70–77.

Cristina, Léa. 1995. "Brasil Supera EUA Nos Preços." *O Globo,* July 1, p. 4.

Da Costa, Maria Teresa Paulino. 2004. "Algumas Considerações Sobre Imigrantes Brasileiros na Jurisdição do Consulado Brasileiro de Nova York." New York: Consulado Brasileiro. Mimeo.

Dalevi, Alessandra. 2001. "Feeling the Pain." *Brazzil,* October, p. 6.

Da Matta, Roberto. 1991. *Carnivals, Rogues, and Heroes: An Interpretation of the Brazilian Dilemma.* Trans. John Drury. Notre Dame, Ind.: University of Notre Dame Press.

Davis, Darién. 1997a. "Disseram Que Eu Voltai Americanizada: Cultural Conflict in the Construction of a Brazilian Identity in the United States, 1930–1970." Paper presented at the meetings of the Brazilian Studies Association, Washington, D.C.

——. 1997b. "The Brazilian-Americans: Demography and Identity of an Emerging Latino Minority." *Latin American Review of Books* (Spring/Fall), pp. 8–15.

DeBiaggi, Sylvia Duarte Dantas. 1996. "Mudança, Crise e Redefinição de Papéis: As Mulheres Brasileiras Lá Fora." *Travessia* (Sept.–Dec.): 24–26.

——. 2002. *Changing Gender Roles: Brazilian Immigrant Families in the U.S.* New York: LFB Scholarly Publishing.

——. 2004. "Homens e Mulheres Mudando em Novos Espaços: Famílias Brasileiras Retornam dos EUA para Brasil." In *Psicologia, E/Imigração e Cultura,* ed. Sylvia Dantas DeBiaggi and Geraldo José De Paiva, 135–64. São Paulo: Casa De Psicólogo Livraria e Editora Ltda.

De Lourenço, Cileine, and Judith McDonnell. 2004. "The Politics of Identity: Brazilian Women Workers in Massachusetts." Paper presented at the meetings of the Latin American Studies Association, Las Vegas, October.

De Oliveira, Patricia. 2005. "An Immigrant's Dream." *Boston Globe*, June 11, op-ed, p. 15.

Dillon, Sam. 2001. "Mexican Immigrants Face New Set of Fears." *New York Times*, October 15, p. 14.

Donohue, Brian. 2005. "Brazilian Influx: As Mexico Border Crossings Increase, New Arrivals Fill Jersey Trades." *Newark Star Ledger*, November 14, p. 1.

Downie, Andrew. 2008. "Boom Times for Brazil's Consumers." *New York Times*, May 24, p. C3.

Duffy, Gary. 2008. "Brazilians Shun 'American Dream.'" BBC, March 25. http://news.bbc.co.uk/2/hi/business/7312408.stm.

Eaton, Leslie, and Edward Wyatt. 2001. "Attacks Hit Low-Pay Jobs Hardest." *New York Times*, November 6, pp. B1, B7.

Economic Policy Institute. 2005. "State of Working America 2004/2005." Washington, D.C.

Economist, The. 2008. "If Redemption Fails, You Can Still Use the Free Bathroom." January 3, p. 31.

Egan, Thomas. 2005. "No Degree, and No Way Back to the Middle." *New York Times*, May 24, p. 15.

Ehrlich, Claudia. 1989. "Beyond Black and White: A Perspective on Racial Attitudes of Paulistas in São Paulo and New York." Senior project, Division of Social Studies, Bard College, Annandale-on-Hudson, New York.

———. 1990. "Stereotypes of Racial Conflict." *Link* 10 (November): 8–9.

Epstein, Aaron. 1997. "Codes in Visa System Mask Bias, Suit Claims." *Miami Herald*, June 5, p. 1.

Espenshade, Thomas J. 1995. "Unauthorized Immigration to the United States." *Annual Review of Sociology* 21:195–216.

Farzad, Roben. 2005. "The Urban Migrants." *New York Times*, July 20, pp. C1, C4.

Feldman-Bianco, Bela. 1992. "Multiple Layers of Time and Space: The Construction of Class, Ethnicity, and Nationalism Among Portuguese Immigrants." In *Towards a Transnational Perspective on Migration: Race, Class, Ethnicity, and Nationalism Reconsidered*, ed. Nina Glick Schiller, Linda Basch, and Cristina Blanc-Szanton, 645: 145–74. New York: Annals of the New York Academy of Sciences.

Fickensher, Lisa. 2005. "Majority of NYC Restaurant Workers Uninsured: Survey." http://www.Newyorkbusiness.com, January 25.

Fisher, Ian. 1996. "Dominican Leader's Triumphant Tour." *New York Times*, October 5, p. 27.

Fix, Michael, and Jeffrey S. Passel. 1994. *Immigration and Immigrants: Setting the Record Straight*. Washington, D.C.: Urban Institute.

Fleischer, Soraya. 2002. *Passando a América a Limpo: O Trabalho de Housecleaners em Boston, Massachusetts*. São Paulo: Annablume Editora.

Foner, Nancy. 1986. "Sex Roles and Sensibilities: Jamaican Women in New York and

London." In *International Migration: The Female Experience*, ed. Rita J. Simon and Caroline B. Brettell, 133–51. Totowa, N.J.: Rowman and Allanheld.

Freedman, Marcia. 1983. "The Labor Market for Immigrants in New York City." *New York Affairs* 7: 94–110.

Freyre, Gilberto. 1964. *The Masters and the Slaves*. Rev. and abridged 2nd ed. New York: Borzoi.

Fundação Instituto Brasileiro de Geografia e Estatística. 2000. "Composição da População por Raça." Rio de Janeiro: Instituto Brasileiro de Geografia e Estatística.

Galvão, Heloísa Maria. 2005. *As Viajantes do Século Vinte*. Rio de Janeiro: H. P. Comunicação Editora.

Gaspari, Elio. 2006. "Inépcia Imperial." *Folha de São Paulo*, December 10.

Gedan, Benjamin. 2002. "Retail Slide Hurts Newcomers: Region's Brazilian Immigrants Hit Hard by Tight Job Market." *Boston Globe* (West Weekly), February 2, p. 1.

Gibson, Annie. 2008. "Brazucas in NOLA: A Cultural Analysis of Brazilian Immigration to New Orleans Post-Katrina." Paper presented at the meetings of the Brazilian Studies Association, New Orleans, March.

Glick Schiller, Nina, Linda Basch, and Cristina Blanc-Szanton. 1992. "Transnationalism: A New Analytic Framework for Understanding Migration." In *Towards a Transnational Perspective on Migration: Race, Class, Ethnicity, and Nationalism Reconsidered*, ed. Nina Glick Schiller, Linda Basch, and Cristina Blanc-Szanton, 645: 1–27. New York: Annals of the New York Academy of Sciences.

Gmelch, George. 1980. "Return Migration." *Annual Review of Anthropology* 9: 135–59.

Gold, Steven J. 1995. *From the Workers' State to the Golden State: Jews from the Former Soviet Union in California*. Boston: Allyn and Bacon.

Gosselin, Peter G. 2004. "If America Is Richer, Why Are Its Families So Much Less Secure?" *Los Angeles Times*, October 10, p. 1.

Goyette, Jared. 2008. "Back to Brazil." *Charleston City Paper*, February 20. http://www.charlestoncitypaper.com/gyrobase/PrintFriendly?oid=oid%3A40675.

Grant, Geraldine. 1981. *New Immigrants and Ethnicity: A Preliminary Research Report on Immigrants in Queens*. New York: Queens College Ethnic Studies Project.

Grasmuck, Sherri, and Patricia R. Pessar. 1992. *Between Two Islands: Dominican International Migration*. Berkeley: University of California Press.

Greenhouse, Steven. 2005. "In $8 Billion Restaurant Industry, a Study Finds Mostly 'Bad Jobs.'" *New York Times*, January 5, p. B7.

Haines, David. 1986. "Vietnamese Refugee Women in the U.S. Labor Force: Continuity or Change?" In *International Migration: The Female Experience*, ed. Rita J. Simon and Caroline B. Brettell, 62–75. Totowa, N.J.: Rowman and Allanheld.

Hondagneu-Sotelo, Pierrette. 1994. *Gendered Transitions: Mexican Experiences of Immigration*. Berkeley: University of California Press.

Hunt, George. 1996. "Raids and Arrests." *America*, July 20, p. 3

Jansen, Tiago, and Carlos Eduardo Siqueira. 2005. "Brazilians Are Everywhere in New England." Paper presented at the National Conference on Brazilian Immigration to the United States, David Rockefeller Center for Latin American Studies, Harvard University, Cambridge, Mass., March 18–19.

Johnson, Mary Helen. 2004. "Undocumented Students in the Boston Brazilian Community." In *Giving Voice to a Nascent Community: Exploring Brazilian Immigration to the U.S. through Research and Practice*, ed. Clémence Jouët-Pastré, Megwen Loveless, and Leticia Braga, Working Paper no. 04/05–2. Cambridge, Mass.: David Rockefeller Center for Latin American Studies, Harvard University.

Johnston, David Cay. 1995. "The Servant Class Is at the Counter." *New York Times*, August 27, sec. 4, pp. 1, 4.

Kammer, Jerry. 2005. "Loophole to America." *San Diego Union-Tribune*, June 4, p. 1.

Kaste, Martin. 2006. "For Poor Brazilians, a Perilous, Illegal Journey to U.S." Reporter's Notebook, National Public Radio, April 16.

Ketcham, Christopher. 2006. "The Devil's Path: On the Trail of the Human-Smuggling Gangs of Arizona." June 14. http://www.christopherketcham.com/.

Kottak, Conrad Phillip. 1990. *Prime Time Society: An Anthropological Analysis of Television and Culture*. Belmont, Calif.: Wadsworth.

Kwong, Peter. 1994. "The Wages of Fear: Undocumented and Unwanted, Fuzhounese Immigrants Are Changing the Face of Chinatown." *Village Voice*, April 26, pp. 25–29.

Lee, Felicia R. 1995. "Slaying Shocks Usually Upbeat Brazilians." *New York Times*, September 21, pp. B1, B3.

Levitt, Peggy. 2001. *The Transnational Villagers*. Berkeley: University of California Press.

Linger, Daniel T. 2001. *No One Home: Brazilian Selves Remade in Japan*. Durham, N.C.: Duke University Press.

Lobo, Arun Peter, and Joseph J. Salvo. 2004. *The Newest New Yorkers 2000*. New York: Population Division, New York City Department of City Planning.

Longman, Jere. 1994. "1 Team, but 150 Million Coaches." *New York Times*, May 10, p. B15.

Lowenstein, Roger. 2006. "The Immigration Equation." *New York Times Magazine*, July 9, p. 36–41.

Lucena, Eliana. 1996. "Estudo Aponta Emigração de um Milhão." *Jornal do Brasil*, March 29.

Luna, Alfons. 2005. "Brasil É o Segundo Destino de Remessas de Emigrantes no Mundo." *Uol Economia*. http://www.noticias.uol.com.br/Economia/Ultnot/Afp/2005/03/22/Ult35u40080.jhtm, accessed on March 22, 2005.

Mahler, Sarah J. 1995. *American Dreaming: Immigrant Life on the Margins*. Princeton, N.J.: Princeton University Press.

Maisonnave, Fabiano. 2005a. "Explode Número de Brasileiros Presos nos EUA." *Folha de São Paulo*, January 16.

———. 2005b. "Igreja dos EUA 'Importa' Padres Brasileiros." *Folha de São Paulo*, January 16.

———. 2005c. "Captura de Brasileiros nos EUA Decuplica." *Folha de São Paulo*, May 5.

———. 2005d. "EUA Têm Recorde de Brasileiros Detidos." *Folha de São Paulo*, October 5.

———. 2006a. "Brasileiros Ilegais Crescem Acima da Média nos EUA." *Folha de São Paulo*, August 19.

———. 2006b. "Brasileiros Deixam de Emigrar via México." *Folha de São Paulo*, November 16.

Maisonnave, Fabiano, and Thiago Guimarães. 2005. "Rota do Tráfico na Guatemala é o Novo Caminho para Atingir EUA." *Folha de São Paulo*, November 30.

Malavolta, Pedro Z. 2005. "Brazil Salaries Have Lost 1/3 of Purchasing Power." *Brazzil*. http://www.brazzilmag.com/content/View/1866/49/, accessed on March 31, 2005.

Marcus, Alan P. 2008. "The Contexts and Consequences of Brazilian Transnational Migration Processes: An Ethnic Geography in Two Countries." Ph.D. diss., Department of Geosciences, University of Massachusetts, Amherst.

Margolis, Mac. 1994. "Brazil and the United States, Stay Away." *The Economist*, October 29, pp. 48, 50.

Margolis, Maxine L. 1990. "An American in Governador Valadares." *The Brasilians* 199 (Sept.): 4.

———. 1994. *Little Brazil: An Ethnography of Brazilian Immigrants in New York City.* Princeton, N.J.: Princeton University Press.

———. 1995a. "Brazilians and the 1990 United States Census: Immigrants, Ethnicity, and the Undercount." *Human Organization* 54(1): 52–59.

———. 1995b. "Transnationalism and Popular Culture: The Case of Brazilian Immigrants in the United States." *Journal of Popular Culture* 29(1): 29–41.

———. 1997. "The Way Things Were: Gender Role Shifts Among Brazilian Immigrants in the United States and Brazil." Paper presented at the 95th annual meeting of the American Anthropological Association, Washington, D.C.

———. 1998a. *An Invisible Minority: Brazilian Immigrants in New York City.* New Immigrants Series. Ed. Nancy Foner. Boston: Allyn and Bacon.

———. 1998b. "Do Looks Matter at the Border?" Letter to the Editor, *New York Times*, January 28, p. 26.

———. 2000. *True to Her Nature: Changing Advice to American Women.* Prospect Heights, Ill.: Waveland Press.

———. 2001. "With New Eyes: Returned International Immigrants in Rio de Janeiro." In *Raízes e Rumos: Perspectivas Interdisciplinares em Estudos Americanos*, ed. Sonia Torres, 239–44. Rio de Janeiro: Editora 7 Letras.

———. 2003. "Brasphobia." Forum on Brasphobia, the Brazilian Rainbow Group, Hunter College-CUNY, New York, December.

———. 2004. "Brazilians in the United States, Canada, Europe, Japan, and Paraguay." In *Encyclopedia of Diasporas*, ed. Melvin Ember, Carol R. Ember, and Ian Skoggard, 602–15. New York: Kluwer Academic/Plenum.

———. 2007. "Becoming Brazucas: Brazilian Identity in the United States." In *The Other Latinos: Central and South Americans in the United States*, ed. José Luis Falconi and José Antonio Mazzotti, 210–27. Cambridge, Mass.: David Rockefeller Center for Latin American Studies, Harvard University.

———. 2008. "September 11 and Transnationalism: The Case of Brazilian Immigrants in the United States." *Human Organization* 67(1): 1–11.

Margolis, Maxine L., Maria E. Bezerra, and Jason Fox. 2001. "Brazil." In *Countries and Their Cultures*, ed. Melvin Ember and Carol R. Ember, 283–301. New York: Macmillan Reference.

Mariz, Cecilia Loreto. 1994. *Coping with Poverty: Pentecostals and Christian Base Communities in Brazil*. Philadelphia: Temple University Press.

Marrow, Helen B. 2002. "To Be or Not to Be (Hispanic or Latino): Brazilians and the Panethnicity Debate." Paper presented at the mini-seminar entitled "Brazilians Outside Brazil: Brasileiros Fora do Brasil," University of Miami, Coral Gables, April 8.

———. 2004. "Coming to Grips with Race: Second-Generation Brazilians in the United States." Paper presented at the meetings of the Brazilian Studies Association, Rio de Janeiro, June 9–12.

Martes, Ana Cristina Braga. 1995. "Relatório Capes/Fulbright." Cambridge. Mimeo.

———. 1996. "Solidariedade e Competição: Acesso ao Mercado de Trablaho e Atuação das Igrejas entre os Imigrantes Brasileiros na Área de Boston." Mimeo.

———. 2000. *Brasileiros nos Estados Unidos: Um Estudo Sobre Imigrantes em Massachusetts*. São Paulo: Editora Paz e Terra.

———. 2007. "Neither Hispanic, Nor Black: We're Brazilian." In *The Other Latinos: Central and South Americans in the United States*, ed. José Luis Falconi and José Antonio Mazzotti, 231–56. Cambridge, Mass.: David Rockefeller Center for Latin American Studies, Harvard University.

Massey, Douglas S. 1988. "Economic Development and International Migration in Comparative Perspective." *Population and Development Review* 14(3): 383–411.

Massey, Douglas S., Jorge Durand, and Nolan J. Malone. 2002. *Beyond Smoke and Mirrors: Mexican Immigration in an Era of Economic Integration*. New York: Russell Sage Foundation.

McKinley, James C., Jr. 2007. "Despite Crackdown, Migrants Stream into South Mexico." *New York Times*, January 28, p. 12.

Menai, Tania. 2007. *Nova York, do Oiapoque ao Chui: Relatos de Brasileiros na Cidade Que Nunca Dorme*. Rio de Janeiro: Casa da Palavra.

Miller, Charlotte I. 1979. "The Function of Middle-Class Extended Family Networks in Brazilian Urban Society." In *Brazil: Anthropological Perspectives*, ed. Maxine L. Margolis and William E. Carter, 305–16. New York: Columbia University Press.

Millman, Joel. 2006. "Immigrant Group Puts a New Spin on Cleaning Niche." *Wall Street Journal*, February 16, p. 1.

Mineo, Liz. 2003. "Illegal Immigrants in a Panic over Scam." *Metro West Daily News*, March 9.

———. 2005. "Brazilian Commission: Group Visits *Metro West*, Boston to Deal with Immigrant Issues." *Metro West Daily News*, October 23.

———. 2006a. "Streets Paved with Dollars." *Metro West Daily News*, December 17.

———. 2006b. "Emigration Disturbs Schools, Students." *Metro West Daily News*, December 20.

Mishel, Lawrence, and Jared Bernstein. 1996. *The State of Working America 1996–97*. Washington, D.C.: Economic Policy Institute.

Moroz, Jennifer. 2005a. "A New Jersey Town, a Brazilian Deluge, Diverging Hopes." *Philadelphia Inquirer*, October 9, p. 1.

———. 2005b. "Flight to the U.S. Brings Brazilians Pain and Promise." *Philadelphia Inquirer*, October 10, p. 6.

Neto, João Sorima, and Ernesto Bernardes. 1996. "A Miami do Brasil." *Veja*, July 17, pp. 50–65.

New York Times. 2008. "One Argument, 12 Million Holes." Editorial, January 18, p. 22.

Nolan, Bruce. 2008. "Many Brazilians Settling in N.O., but for How Long?" *Times-Picayune*, January 19, p. 1.

O'Dougherty, Maureen. 1995. "International Bargain Shopping: Consumption and Brazilian Middle Class Identity in the 1990s." Paper presented at the 19th International Congress of the Latin American Studies Association, Washington, D.C.

O Globo. 1995. "Classe Média Passou Logo da Euforia à Inadimplência." July 1, p. 4.

O'Leary, Mary E. 2005. "Danbury March Shows Support for Immigrants." *New Haven Register*, June 13, p. 1.

Papademetriou, Demetrios G., and Nicholas DiMarzio. 1986. *Undocumented Aliens in the New York Metropolitan Area*. New York: Center for Migration Studies.

Passel, Jeffrey S., Randolph Capps, and Michael E. Fix. 2004. "Undocumented Immigrants: Facts and Figures." Washington, D.C.: Urban Institute Immigration Studies Program.

Peluso, Luciana, and Simone Goldberg. 1995. "Heróis da Sobrevivência." *Isto É*, December 7, pp. 124–29.

Pereira, Néli. 2008. "Boom ainda não atrai imigrantes de volta ao Brasil." BBC Brasil, March 24. http://www.bbc.co.uk/portuguese/reporterbbc/story/2008/03/080319_imigracaoboomeconomia_np.shtml.

Pessar, Patricia R. 1985. "When the Birds of Passage Want to Roost: An Exploration of the Role of Gender in Dominican Settlement in the U.S." In *Women and Change in Latin America*, ed. June Nash and Helen I. Safa, 273–94. South Hadley, Mass.: Bergin and Harvey.

———. 1995. "The Elusive Enclave: Ethnicity, Class, and Nationality among Latino Entrepreneurs in Greater Washington, D.C." *Human Organization* 54(4): 383–92.

Pickel, Mary Lou. 2000. "Brazilians Catch Wave to Atlanta." *Atlanta Journal-Constitution*, September 18, p. B1.

Piore, Michael J. 1979. *Birds of Passage: Migrant Labor and Industrial Societies*. New York: Cambridge University Press.

———. 1986. "The Shifting Grounds for Migration." *Annals of the American Academy of Political and Social Science* 485: 23–33.

Porter, Eduardo. 2005a. "Illegal Immigrants Are Bolstering Social Security with Billions." *New York Times*, April 5, p. 1.

———. 2005b. "Social Security: Migrants Offer Numbers for Fee." *New York Times*, June 7, p. 1.

Portes, Alejandro, ed. 1990. *The New Second Generation*. New York: Russell Sage.

Portes, Alejandro, and Robert L. Bach. 1985. *Latin Journey: Cuban and Mexican Immigrants in the United States*. Berkeley: University of California Press.

Powell, Michael. 2005. "New Tack Against Illegal Immigrants: Trespassing Charges." *Washington Post*, June 10, p. 1.

Preston, Julia. 2007. "Judge Voids Ordinance on Illegal Immigrants." *New York Times*, July 27, p. 14.

———. 2008a. "Fearing Deportation but Clinging to Life and Homes in the U.S." *New York Times*, January 18, p. 14.

———. 2008b. "In Reversal, Courts Uphold Local Immigration Laws." *New York Times*, February 10, p. 22.

Reel, Monte. 2006. "Losing Its Young to an American Dream." *Washington Post*, November 14, p. 22.

Repak, Terry A. 1995. *Waiting on Washington: Central American Workers in the Nation's Capital*. Philadelphia: Temple University Press.

Resende, Rosana. 2002. "Tropical Brazucas: A Preliminary Study of Brazilians in South Florida." Paper presented at the mini-seminar entitled "Brazilians Outside Brazil: Brasileiros Fora do Brasil," University of Miami, Coral Gables, April 8.

———. 2005. "Fragile Threads." *Hemisphere* 15 (Summer): 4–6.

Ribeiro, Gustavo Lins. 1999. "O Que Faz O Brasil, *Brazil*: Jogos Identitários em San Francisco." In *Cenas Do Brasil Migrante*, ed. Rosana Rocha Reis and Teresa Sales, 45–85. São Paulo: Boitempo Editorial.

Rohter, Larry. 2005. "Brazilians Streaming into U.S. through Mexican Border." *New York Times*, June 30, p. 3.

———. 2006. "At Long Last, a Neglected Language Is Put on a Pedestal." *New York Times*, October 23, p. 4.

Ruiz, Albor. 2005. "Restaurant Workers Are Poorly Served." *Daily News*, suburban section, January 27, p. 4.

Safa, Helen I. 1995. "Economic Restructuring and Gender Subordination." *Latin American Perspectives* 22(2): 33–51.

Sales, Teresa. 1998. "Constructing an Ethnic Identity: Brazilian Immigrants in Boston, Mass." *Migration World* 26(5): 15–21.

———. 1999. "Identitidade Étnica Entre Imigrantes Brasileiros na Região de Boston, EUA." In *Cenas Do Brasil Migrante*, ed. Rosana Rocha Reis and Teresa Sales, 15–44. São Paulo: Boitempo Editorial.

———. 2003. *Brazilians Away from Home*. New York: Center for Migration Studies.

———. 2007. "Second Generation Brazilian Immigrants in the United States." In *The Other Latinos: Central and South Americans in the United States*, ed. José Luis Falconi and José Antonio Mazzotti, 195–211. Cambridge, Mass.: David Rockefeller Center for Latin American Studies, Harvard University.

Salgado, Eduardo. 2001. "Eles Fogem Da Bagunça." *Veja*, July 18, pp. 94–100.

———. 2002. "O Eldorado Brilha Menos." *Veja*, January 16.

Sassen-Koob, Saskia. 1986. "New York City: Economic Restructuring and Immigration." *Development and Change* 17: 85–119.

Schmitt, Eric. 1996. "Giuliani Criticizes G.O.P. and Dole on Immigration." *New York Times*, June 7, p. B3.

Schneider, Dorothee. 1998. "'I Know All about Emma Lazarus': Nationalism and Its

Contradictions in Congressional Rhetoric of Immigration Restriction." *Cultural Anthropology* 13(1): 82–99.

Scudeler, Cristina. 1999. "Imigrantes Valadarenses no Mercado de Trabalho dos EUA." In *Cenas do Brasil Migrante*, ed. Rosana Rocha Reis and Teresa Sales, 193–232. São Paulo: Boitempo.

Shenon, Philip. 1997. "Judge Denounces U.S. Visa Policies Based on Race and Looks." *New York Times*, January 23, pp. 1, 9.

———. 1998. "State Department Illegally Denying Visas, Judge Says." *New York Times*, January 23, p. 1.

Shokeid, Moshe. 1988. *Children of Circumstances: Israeli Emigrants in New York*. Ithaca, N.Y.: Cornell University Press.

Simon, Rita J., and Margo Corona DeLey. 1986. "Undocumented Mexican Women: Their Work and Personal Experiences." In *International Migration: The Female Experience*, ed. Rita J. Simon and Caroline B. Brettell, 113–32. Totowa, N.J.: Rowman and Allanheld.

Sims, Calvin. 1995. "The South American Art of Name-Calling." *New York Times*, July 30, p. E4.

Siqueira, C. Eduardo, and Cileine de Lourenço. 2004. "Brazilian Immigration to Massachusetts: Newcomers to a Foreign Land." Paper presented at the meetings of the Latin American Studies Association, Las Vegas, October.

Siqueira, Sueli. 2005. "Projeto de Retorno e Investimento dos Imigrantes Valadarenses nos EUA." Paper presented at the National Congress on Brazilian Immigration to the United States, David Rockefeller Center for Latin American Studies, Harvard University, Cambridge, Mass., March 18–19.

Sontag, Deborah. 1994. "U.S. Arrests 3 in Immigration Marriage Fraud." *New York Times*, July 22, pp. 1, B2.

Sotero, Paulo. 2006. "Brasileiros se Mobilizam nos EUA." *O Estado de São Paulo*, April 23.

Souza (Galvão), Heloisa. 2004. "Brazilians in Boston: Before and After 9/11." Paper presented at the symposium entitled "What About the Other Latinos? Central and South Americans in the United States," David Rockefeller Center for Latin American Studies, Harvard University, Cambridge, Mass., April 5.

Stana, Richard M. 2007. "US-Visit Program Faces Operational, Technological, and Management Challenges." Testimony before the Committee on Homeland Security, House of Representatives. http://www.209.85.165.104/search?q=cache:ws9gjaBsmAJ:www.gao.gov/new.items/d07632t.pdf+%22US+Visit+Program%22&hl=en&ct=clnk&cd=8&gl=us.

Strategier, Valerie. 2006. "Made in Brazil, Imagining America: Brazilian Immigrants in New York City." M.A. thesis, Department of Social Anthropology, Utrecht University.

Suarez, Ana Veciana. 2003. "Viva o Brasil! Brazilian Community Growing Strong in Broward." *Miami Herald*, April 9, p. E1.

Suárez-Orozco, Carola, and Marcelo Suárez-Orozco. 1995. "Migration: Generational Discontinuities and the Making of Latino Identities." In *Ethnic Identity: Creation,*

Conflict, and Accommodation, ed. Lola Romanucci-Ross and George DeVos, 321–47. Walnut Creek, Calif.: Altamira Press.

———. 2001. *Children of Immigration*. Cambridge, Mass.: Harvard University Press.

Suro, Roberto. 2006. "America's Immigration Quandary." Pew Hispanic Center. http://www.pewhispanic.org/reports/report.php?ReportID=63, accessed March 30, 2006.

Thurow, Lester. 1995. "Why Their World Might Crumble." *New York Times Magazine*, November 19, pp. 78–79.

Vasquez, Manuel, Lúcia Ribeiro, and José Claudio S. Alves. 2008. "Congregations as Spaces of Empowerment and Disempowerment Among Brazilians in the New South." Paper presented at "Brazilian-Americans in Georgia and Beyond: A Multi-Disciplinary Symposium." University of Georgia and Georgia State University, Athens and Atlanta, April.

Veja. 1995a. "Multinactional da Fé." April 19, pp. 92–94.

———. 1995b. "Os Preços Muito Loucos da Era do Real." July 19, pp. 18–24.

Waldinger, Roger. 1989. "Immigration and Urban Change." *Annual Review of Sociology* 15: 211–32.

———. 1993. *Black/Immigrant Competition Re-assessed: New Evidence from Los Angeles*. Los Angeles: UCLA, Department of Sociology.

———. 1996. *Still the Promised City? New Immigrants and African-Americans in Post-Industrial New York*. Cambridge, Mass.: Harvard University Press.

Weis, Luiz. 2007. "Fazendo a América com o Escovão." *Estado de São Paulo*, March 28.

White, Cassandra. 2008. "Concepts of Class and Citizenship in the Brazilian Community in Atlanta." Paper presented at the meetings of the Brazilian Studies Association, New Orleans, March.

Woolhouse, Megan. 2005. "A Valedictorian without a Visa." *Boston Globe*, June 3, pp. A1, B5.

Wright, Robert. 1995. "Who's Really to Blame?" *Time*, November 6, p. 32.

Yahoo News. 2005. "Non-Mexicans Arrested at U.S. Border Nearly Doubled." http://www./P238.News.Mud.Yahoo.Com/S/Nm/Security_Immigration_Dc, accessed July 12, 2005.

Yoon, In-Jin. 1991. "The Changing Significance of Ethnic and Class Resources in Immigrant Businesses: The Case of Korean Immigrant Business in Chicago." *International Migration Review* 25(2): 120–30.

Zentgraf, Kristine. 1995. "Household Composition, Decision to Settle, and the Changing Political Economic Context: Central Americans in Los Angeles." Paper presented at the 19th International Congress of the Latin American Studies Association, Washington, D.C.

Index

Adolescents, jobs and, 110
African Americans, 100
Age, 35-36
Airports, control at, 126
Alienation, 72
Amazon, 95
American(s): born children, 110; Brazilian vs., employers, 81; Brazilian vs., personality, 73; in Governor Valadares, 2; ignorance about Brazil, 93-95; middle class, 21, 55
American Community Survey, 5
Amnesty Program, 132n3
Anxiety, 77-78
Apparel industry, 43
Astoria (Queens, N.Y.), 4, 5, 62, 66
Atlanta, 3, 4, 86

Baixada, 33
Bankruptcy, 115
Behavior, change of, 79-80, 118, 126
Benefits, lack of, 40, 41, 44, 52
Betrayal, 79-80
Border control, 125; tightening of, 127
Boston, 31, 33
Brazil: American ignorance about, 93-95; income in, 10, 11, 27, 43; misrepresentation of, 94. See also "Little Brazil"
Brazilian: American vs., employers, 81; American vs., personality, 73; children, 110; communities, xii, 2, 3-4, 6-7; economy, x, 1, 9-10, 115, 117; family life, 72; imported goods, 67; neighborhoods in New York, 4-5; non-Brazilian immigrants, 4-5, 76, 80, 81, 102, 104-5, 109, 127; businesses, 56, 62-63, 66, 70-71, 82; popularity of things, 93; professions of, immigrants, 10, 24-25. See also immigrant(s)
Brazilian Immigrant Center, 125, 132n3
Brazilian Independence Day Fair, 84, 85
Brazilian Rainbow Group, 81, 132n3
Brazilians: in Consular Districts, 6; foreign-born, 6; invisibility of, 92, 93; Japanese, 97, 133n3; media coverage of, 92-93; professions of, immigrants, 10, 24-25; September 11th impact on, 121-26; as sojourners, 7, 62, 70, 83, 106, 107, 108, 130. See also immigrant(s)
Brazilian Street Fair, 67, 68
Brazilian Times, 122
Brazucas, xi, 57
Bureaucracy, 81

Bush, George W. (U.S. president), 95, 125
Business(es): Brazilian owned, 56, 62-63, 66, 70-71, 82; domestic service as, 70-71
Buying power, 74

Cable News Network (CNN), 39
California, xii, 2, 3
Cape Cod (Mass.), 4
Capoeira, 62
Cardoso, Fernando Henrique (Brazilian president), 94, 95
Carnegie Hall, 62
Catskill Mountains, 2
Center for Brazilian Immigrants, 115
Chertoff, Michael (U.S. director of homeland security), 125
Chicago, 3
Child care, 26, 39, 49, 51, 52
Children: American born, 110; Brazilian, 110; education of immigrant, 111. See also child care
Church(es): Catholic, 84, 85; evangelical, 84, 85-86; immigrants aided by, 86; Portuguese-speaking, services, 85; solidarity through evangelical, 86-87; unifying value of, 84, 86; Universal, 87-88, 132n6
Citizenship, 133n2
Clothing, 46, 73-74, 132n2
Clubs, 83
CNN. See Cable News Network
Communication, 107
Community(ies): cohesion of, 80-81, 82; destination city and "sending," 31; education and "sending," 31; lacking social/physical, 82; leaders, 82; locations of Brazilian, xii, 2, 3-4, 6-7; organizations, 80-81; "sending," 24, 36; "sending" and class association, 30-31; solidarity, 84
Commuting, 114
Competition, 34, 35
Connecticut, xii, 3, 6, 31, 123
Construction work, 57, 101, 126
Consumerism, 111; patterns of, 128-29
Contact(s): with home, 107-8; social, 29, 30
Corruption, 132n2
Cost of living, 75
Counterfeit documents, 17-18, 48
Crime, 55; rise in, 20
Cultural pride, 96
Culture: clash, x; shock, 73, 115

Data, demographic, xii, 5-6
Delusion, 75
Department of Homeland Security, 7, 8, 17, 18, 44, 48, 76, 125, 131n3, 132n1
Department of Labor, 51
Deportation, 76; of OTMs, 125
Depression, 128
Development, industrial/agricultural, 129
Discontent, 115
Discord, 102-3
Discrimination, 14, 122
Disillusionment, 115
Distancing, between immigrants, 79-80
Dobbs, Lou, 39
Document(s): counterfeit, 17-18, 48; obtaining travel, 29-30
Dollar, value of, 113
Domestic service, 35, 44, 49, 101; as business, 70-71; disadvantages of, 52; live-in, 50, 51; social status and, 69-70
Dreams, deceptive, 74-75
Driver's license, 113, 133n1; legal status and, 123; obtaining, 122-23

Economist, The, 15
Economy, 116, 117, 130; Brazilian, x, 1, 9-10, 115, 117; changes in U.S., 20-21; globalization of, 21; informal, 40, 44, 52; middle class and, 10; of New York, 116, 117; of time, 11; U.S., ix, 74
Education, ix, x, 11, 34, 37, 128; college, 10, 21, 111; cost of, 111-12; of immigrant children, 111; of immigrants, 25-26, 27, 129; middle class and, x, 11, 23, 37; of non-Brazilian immigrants; "sending" communities and, 31
Elite, 33, 39, 131n2
Ellis Island Museum, 92
Emigration, 10; facilitation of, 32; from Governador Valadares, 2-3, 11; motivation for, x, 8-12; rate of, 3. See also immigration; migration
Employers: American vs. Brazilian, 81; illegal immigrants hired by, 40, 41, 42, 44, 47, 48, 132n4; relationship of employees with, 73; sanctions against, 48
Employment: ascending, ladder, 49, 54; networks, 42, 54, 83; unemployment and, 42, 118, 121, 129. See also job(s); wage(s)
Entrapment, feeling of, 128
Entry: denial of, 127; routes of, xii, 1; via Guatemala, 126; via Mexico, 16, 27, 92, 123-25
Ethical standards, softening of, 79, 80
Ethnicity, 7-8, 34, 35, 68, 96, 99; ambivalence of, 81; cohesion/solidarity of, 80-81, 82
E-Verify, 132n4
Expenses, minimizing/sharing, 45, 46
Exploitation, 50, 82

Family. See relatives
Fear, 76, 77-78, 98, 122

Financial: pressure for immigrants, 34-35; support for relatives, 28, 32; support from friends, 32; women's, independence, 101-2, 103, 104, 109
Florida, 3, 4, 6, 84
Food, native, 89, 132n8
Freeloader, 44
Friends, 12, 16, 17, 18, 30, 31; financial support from, 32; leisure time with, 90

Gender: improvement in, relations, 104-5, 109; labor recruitment and, 100-101; ratio of immigrants, 35; return home and, 109; shift in, roles, 101-3, 109. See also women
Giuliani, Rudolph (mayor), 132n4
Globalization, of economy, 21
Go-go dancing, 60, 61; monopoly on, 58, 59
Governador Valadares, 30, 31, 32, 36, 57, 59, 65; Americans in, 2; emigration from, 2-3, 11
Graça Lima, José Alfredo (ambassador), xii
Green card, 51, 58, 77, 78, 107, 109, 112, 118, 133n2; transnationalism and, 126
Guatemala, entry via, 126

Health insurance, 21, 44
Hispanics, 4, 7, 8, 42, 78, 95-98, 99, 133n2
Homesickness, 115
Hotel and Restaurant Employees International Union, 121
Household(s): income, 21-22, 23; no family, 19
Houston, 3
Human warmth, lack of, 73

ICE. See Immigration and Customs Enforcement
Identity, 96, 97, 99
Immigrant(s): anti-immigrant sentiment, 77, 130; blame, 20-22; churches aiding, 86; distancing between, 79-80; education of, 25-26, 27, 129; education of, children, 111; education of non-Brazilian, 29; employers hiring illegal, 40, 41, 42, 44, 47, 48, 132n4; entrepreneurial niche of, 62; financial pressure for, 34-35; gain of host country from, 130; identifying, 16; income of, 2, 27, 41, 42, 43, 45, 52, 56; jobs of, 38, 44, 49, 50-64; jobs taken away by, 39-40; labor market and, 38-39; legal, 44; longtime, 128; network of, 17, 30, 42, 54, 59; non-Brazilian, 4-5, 76, 80, 81, 102, 104-5, 109, 127; organized funding for, 27-28; professions of Brazilian, 10, 24-25; sex ratio of, 35; social classes of Brazilian, 25; solidarity and, 34-35; split between old and new, 34; travel and, 126-27, 129
Immigration: continued, 117-18; illegal/undocumented, ix, x, xi, 7, 8, 40, 41, 44, 47, 76, 123, 125, 132n3; motivation for, 8-12; passing through, 15-16; "polluting" influence of, 20; priorities after, 17-20; reform legislation, 18,

113; resources for, 13, 29. *See also* emigration; migration
Immigration and Customs Enforcement (ICE), 48
Immigration and Naturalization Service, 69, 132n1
Immigration Reform and Control Act (IRCA), 47, 48, 101, 132n3
Income: in Brazil, 10, 11, 27, 43; high, elite, 39; household, 21-22, 23; of immigrants, 2, 27, 41, 42, 43, 45, 52, 56; inequalities in, 21-22; through shoeshining, 60; tax, 44. *See also* wage(s)
Independence: Brazilian, Day Fair, 84, 85; women's financial, 101-2, 103, 104, 109
Indifference, 96
Indignity, 15
Inequality, 70
Inflation, 74, 113; middle class and, 9, 10, 115
Information, 29; networks, 30
Informers, 79, 82
Invisibility, of Brazilians, 92, 93
IRCA. *See* Immigration Reform and Control Act
Isolation, 50, 72

Japanese. *See under* Brazilians
Jeitinho, 81-82
Job(s), x, 6; of adolescents, 110; attraction of low wage, 42-43; changing, 46-47; concealing nature of, 70; of immigrants, 38, 44, 49, 50-64; immigrants taking away, 39-40; low wage, 39, 40, 41, 43, 129, 130; low-wage, and middle class, 70; opportunities, 29; security, 21, 40, 52, 130; service sector, 38-39, 40; stealing of, 80; working two, 45, 75
John Paul II (pope), 85

Katrina (hurricane), 4
Kottak, Conrad P., 83

Labor: contractors, 57; high turnover, 40; imported, 38; low cost, 48; manual, 69; market and immigrants, 38-39; marriage and division of, 103, 104, 105, 109; recruitment and gender, 100-101; skilled/unskilled, 53, 57; supply changes, 39; surplus, 129; unions, 40, 57
Labor surplus, 129
Labor unions, 40
Landscaping, 57, 126
Language skills, 37, 40, 52, 55, 72, 73, 111. *See also* Portuguese
Law enforcement, 73
Layoffs, following September 11, 2001, 121
Legal status, 34, 44, 51, 73, 107, 109; driver's license and, 123; of immigrants, 44; through marriage, 78; return home and, 112
Legislation, immigration reform, 18, 113

Leisure (time), 62, 91, 118-19; cost of, 46, 88, 89; outdoor, 89-90; with relatives/friends, 90
Lincoln Center, 62
"Little Brazil," 4, 33, 62, 66, 82, 84, 89, 92, 132n4
Live-ins, 50-51
Living conditions, x, 18-20, 119
Loneliness, 37, 72
Los Angeles, 4, 38

Macedo, Edir, 87
Manual labor, 69
Mariel boatlift, 42
Marriage, 36; breakup of, 102-3; division of labor in, 103, 104, 105, 109; legalization through, 78
Martes, Cristina, 51, 70, 83, 85, 86, 117
Massachusetts, xii, 3, 4, 5, 7, 31, 51, 77, 110, 111
Media, 12, 74; coverage of Brazilians, 92-93; exposure, 128
Mexico: entry via, 16, 27, 92, 123-25; visa requirements for, 125, 126
Mica industry, 2
Middle class, 12, 28, 29, 69, 130; advantages for, 29-30; American, 21, 55; definition of/identifying, 24-25; economy and, 10; education and, x, 11, 23, 37; inflation and, 9, 10, 115; living standards of, 129; low-wage work and, 70; race and, 99. *See also* social class(es)
Migration: chain, 36-37, 37; international, 128-30; secondary, 6; sequencing of, by social class, 30-32; transnational, 107, 108, 114; women's status and, 102; yo-yo, 114, 115, 126. *See also* emigration; immigration
Minas Gerais, 2, 11, 17, 26, 31, 32, 131n1
Mineiros, 32-33
Minimum wage, 40, 43, 44.75, 131n1
Miranda, Carmen, 94
Mobility, 71, 111, 130; downward, 70; upward, 54
Modernity, 12
Money, pursuit of, 74-76, 80, 83, 88
Monopoly, on go-go dancing/shoe shining, 58, 59

Nascimento, Milton, 88, 132n7
National identity card, 76
Network(s), 37; employment, 42, 54, 83; of immigrants, 17, 30, 42, 54, 59; information, 30; social, 81
New Jersey, xii, 2, 3, 6, 27, 31
New Orleans, 3, 4
New York: Brazilian neighborhoods in, 4-5; economy of, 116, 117
New York Times, 91, 92, 121, 133n1

Operation Texas Hold 'Em, 125
OTMs (Other Than Mexicans), 17, 124; deportation of, 125

Paraguay, x
Pennsylvania, 6
Pension, 21
Performing arts, native, 62-63, 84, 89
Personality, Brazilian vs. American, 73
Personal references, 52
Philadelphia, 3
Portuguese, 85, 93, 95, 96
Poverty, ix, x, 20
Prejudice, 07, 96
Privacy, 18-19, 72-73
Professions, of Brazilian immigrants, 10, 24-25
Puleiros, 19

Quality of life, 73, 74, 119, 128
Queens (borough), 4, 89, 92

Race, 34, 96, 100; middle class and, 99; social class and, 26, 99
Radio call cars, 45, 54, 62
Raids, 76-77
Reagan, Ronald (U.S. president), 93
Real ID Act, 2005, 123
Real Plan, 10
Recession, 113
Relatives, 12, 16, 17, 18, 30, 31; assistance from, 83; financial support for, 28, 32; leisure time with, 90; separation from, 72; sponsoring of, 36-37
Remittances, 28, 32, 35, 62, 75, 108; importance of, 129
Resende, Rosana, 81
Resources, for immigration, 13, 29
Restaurant work, 40, 44, 45, 49, 71, 132n5; positions in, 53-54
Retirement, 128
Return home, 105, 107, 118, 127-28; gender and, 109; ideology of, 119; legal status and, 112; reasons for, 112-13; after September 11, 2001, 122. *See also* sojourners
Rice, Condoleezza (U.S. secretary of state), 95
Rio de Janeiro, xi, 5, 9, 14, 16, 30, 31, 33, 131n1

Sales, Teresa, 110
San Diego, 4
San Francisco, 4
São Paulo, 5, 10, 14, 30, 31, 33, 43
Saudades, 37, 69
Savings, 108, 119; plans for, 75
Selfishness, 79-80
September 11, 2001, xii, 13, 16, 48, 77, 86, 116, 117, 132n1, 133n2; impact on Brazilians, 121-26; layoffs following, 121; obtaining tourist visa after, 123; return home after, 122; transnationalism and, 126-28
Settlement, 118-19; shift to permanent, 127
Shoeshining, 42, 44, 45, 49, 52; income through, 60; monopoly on, 58, 59

Smuggling, 124
Soccer, World Cup of, 90-91, 92
Social class(es), 34, 97, 100; of Brazilian immigrants, 25; chasm, 33; identifying, 23-24, 25, 28; interaction of, 99; makeup, 29; migration sequencing by, 30-32; race and, 26, 99; "sending" communities and, 30-31; shifts in, makeup, 26-27. *See also* middle class; working class
Social Security: card, 17-18, 56, 77, 122; counterfeit, cards, 48; tax, 44
Social status, 96-97; decline in, 69, 70-71; domestic service and, 69-70; migration and women's, 102; women's degraded, 70
Social welfare, 73
Sojourners: Brazilians as, 7, 62, 70, 83, 106, 107, 108, 130. *See also* return home
Solidarity: community, 84; ethnic, 80-81, 82; through evangelical church, 86-87; immigrants and, 34-35
South Carolina, 6
Stereotype(s), 99, 100; socioeconomic, 33-34
Street vending, 55
Superiority, 96-97
Surplus labor, 129
Sweatshops, raids on, 76-77

Target earners, 11, 112
Tax(es): income, 44; payroll, 45; Social Security, 44
Terrorism, 48
Time (magazine), 57
Tradition, 83
Training, reduced cost of, 42
Transnationalism: benefits of, 130; global, 128; green card and, 126; migration and, 107, 108, 114; September 11, 2001, and, 126-28
Transportation, 107
Travel: immigrants and, 126-27, 129; obtaining, documents, 29-30
Travel agencies, 62

Unemployment, 118, 121, 129; rate, 42
Unions. *See* labor
United States: 1990 and 2000 census, x, 5, 7, 98; changes in, economy, 20-21; economy, ix, 74; return to, 114-16. *See also* American(s)
Unity, 34, 99
University degrees, 10
U.S.-Visit, 76, 131n3

Veja (newsmagazine), 33, 57, 122
Visa(s), ix, 76; Mexican, requirements, 125, 126; qualifying for, 13-15; tourist, 1, 7, 17, 27, 28, 30, 65, 116; tourist, after September 11, 2001, 123

Wage(s), 10, 11; low, attraction of, 42-43; deterioration of, 21; low-wage jobs, 39, 40, 41, 43, 129, 130; low-wage jobs and middle class, 70; minimum, 40, 43, 44, 75, 131n1; off the books, 44, 52; structure, 41-42; women working for low, 133n4. *See also* income
Washington, D.C., 3, 38
Weather, 56
Women: degraded status of, 70; financial independence of, 101-2, 103, 104, 109; low-wage work of, 133n4; migration and status of, 102; working, 21, 22, 26, 44, 49, 50, 51, 59. *See also* gender
Worker's compensation, 44
Working class, 26, 27, 28, 32. *See also* social class(es)
Work papers, 18, 37, 40, 43; validity of, 48
World Trade Center, 121, 122
World War II, 2, 21

Maxine L. Margolis is a professor emerita of anthropology and Latin American studies at the University of Florida, Gainesville, and an adjunct senior research scholar of the Institute of Latin American Studies, Columbia University. She is the author of *Little Brazil: An Ethnography of Brazilian Immigrants in New York City* (1994) and *True to Her Nature: Changing Advice to American Women* (2000).